Second Edition

Hiring Right:

A Business Blueprint™ for Lower Turnover and Higher Profits

Pat Kelley, MS, SPHR

**Hiring Right: A Business Blueprint™ for Lower
Turnover and Higher Profits
Second Edition**

© Copyright 2014, 2004 by Pat Kelley

All rights reserved. No part of this book may be reproduced or transmitted in any form or by any means, electronic or mechanical, including photocopying, recording or by any information storage and retrieval system without the express written permission from the author, except for the inclusion of brief quotations in a review.

Notice

This book is designed to provide information with regard to the subject matter covered. It is sold with the understanding that the publisher and author are not engaged in rendering legal or accounting services. If legal or other expert assistance is required, the services of a licensed professional should be sought. The author and the publisher shall have neither liability nor responsibility to any person or entity with respect to any loss or damage caused, or alleged to be caused, directly or indirectly, by the information contained in this book.

The cases and incidents related in this book are real. They are the experiences of the author over more than 43 years in Human Resources. However, the names of the people involved have been changed to protect their privacy. Any resemblance to real persons living or dead is purely coincidence.

ISBN:1502863944

Contents

Introduction
    The Cost of Turnover

Part One: A Blueprint for Basic Hiring Skills

Chapter One
    Develop a Profile of the "Ideal" Employee
        Mistake Number One
        Mistake Number Two
        Mistake Number Three
        Profile the job first
        Research the Job History
        Complete a Personality Profile

Chapter Two
    Recruiting and Screening Applicants
        Promotion from within
        Employee referrals
        Networking
        Applications on file
        Trade publications
        The Internet
        Schools and colleges
        Employment agencies
        "Free" Services
        Agencies that charge fees
        Executive search firms
        Taking and screening applications
        Testing

Chapter Three
    Conduct a valid screening interview
        Use a patterned interview
        Step One
        Step Two
        Step Three
        Step Four
        Step Five
        Step Six

Professional, Management and Executive level positions
Developing Interviewing questions

Chapter Four
Employment Law in Hiring
How to prevent problems in hiring
Interviewing danger zones

Chapter Five
What's next?
New hire training
The work environment

Part Two: Business Blueprints™

Blueprint One
A Business Blueprint™ for Hiring Office Clerical Workers
Office Clerical Newspaper Ad
Office Clerical Job Profile
Office Clerical Patterned Interview
Office Clerical Orientation Checklist

Blueprint Two

A Business Blueprint™ for Hiring Entry Level Labor
Entry Level Labor Job Profile
Entry Level Labor Patterned Interview
Entry Level Labor Orientation Checklist

Blueprint Three
A Business Blueprint™ for Hiring Technical Workers
Technical Job Profile
Technical Patterned Interview
Technical Orientation Checklist

Blueprint Four
  A Business Blueprint™ for Hiring Sales Staff
    Sales Job Profile
    Sales Patterned Interview
    Sales Candidate Offer Letter
    Sales Orientation Checklist

Blueprint Five
  A Business Blueprint™ for Hiring Management Staff
    Management Job Profile
    Management Patterned Interview
    Management Candidate Offer Letter
    Management Orientation Checklist

Resources

Hiring Right   Pat Kelley

Introduction

The noisy babble of the Chamber of Commerce "business after hours" get-together rolled over me as I signed in, handed over five dollars and pressed a nametag to my lapel. After several years of retirement, I wondered if the business owners and managers I hoped to meet would still be as cynical about hiring and retaining employees as they had been when I wrote the original edition of *Hiring Right*, in 2004.

And how would the "great recession" of 2008-2012 have affected hiring and retaining employees, if at all?

These were the questions I wanted to answer when I embarked on the Second Edition of *Hiring Right: A Business Blueprint for Lower Turnover and Higher Profits*. So what did I learn? I learned that the need to reduce turnover is as great as ever—in fact, during a time when unemployed workers are still plentiful and jobs are still few and far between, it's more important than ever to do a great job of recruiting, screening and hiring employees who have the *ability* to do the job, and the *willingness* to do the job. We also call that *"can do" and "will do."* Or we often think of those qualities as having both the *skills* and the *attitude* to do the job.

If we miss the mark on our recruiting, screening and hiring, we end up with employees who are willing—and able, in many cases—to go down the street to an employer who is paying fifty cents more per hour, or who offers more paid vacation days.

In 2004, employers were complaining about the "revolving door" of applicants who begged for a job, said they were willing to work any shift and any kind of job, then barely completed New Employee Orientation before they left and never returned again. That is largely still the case, according to the business owners and managers with whom I've visited. These managers are tired of seeing "desperate" applicants who promise whatever they think managers want to hear, then either never show up for work, fail their pre-employment drug and reference checks, or come in with an entitlement attitude and make demands about working conditions or benefits that our companies are not prepared to make.

Ten years ago, a common complaint was "People just don't want to work. They don't know what it's like to be hungry. All they're interested in is how much time off they can get and how long they have to work before they can get some benefits."

I still hear the same complaints today, and am increasingly frustrated that in spite of my near-constant preaching, most companies are still not using effective recruiting, screening and hiring techniques, and their employee turnover is still bleeding the companies dry.

The Cost of Turnover

Most business owners and some business managers know that hiring costs go right to the bottom line. Hiring costs are overhead, pure and simple. If you make a product, you can put the actual cost of labor into your product price and recover most of your cost. If what you sell is a service, overhead is included in the rates you charge. But if your overhead is too high you price yourself out of the market. There is no way to pass along most of your overhead costs, so you pay them out of your gross margin and hope there is enough there to cover them. In other words, every dollar you spend on turnover is one less dollar that goes into the profit column. It's a cost you simply cannot afford.

Research by the Society for Human Resource Management (SHRM) has proven that it costs between one-and two-and-a-half times the average annual pay to replace an employee who leaves your company, regardless the reason. For example, let's say you pay your front counter customer service clerk ten dollars an hour ($10), and the clerk works full-time, or 2,080 hours per year. That's a total of $20,800 a year, plus benefits and overtime, if necessary.

That clerk has been with you for two years and understands all the policies. She knows most of the customers, and is a whiz at filling orders. If she should leave, you cannot leave the front desk position unfilled so you immediately start recruiting. The position is not filled by the time the clerk actually leaves, so you call a temporary agency for help. Now, in addition to the $10 per hour, you have to pay a 45% mark-up to the agency, pushing your cost up to $10.45.

You spend several hours training the temporary in the very basic duties of the job, all the while grimacing at the added cost—and this lady doesn't even begin to understand a tenth of what the former clerk did. What a waste of money!

After just one day on the job, the temporary worker decides the job is just too complicated for her, and doesn't return to work.

You call the agency and they fill the job again, but now you're spending so much time training temporaries that you don't have time to recruit and interview potential full-time employees.

Costs are even higher for professional level employees. A CPA firm pays entry level accountants with college degrees a starting salary of $45,000. Because of the higher costs involved in recruiting, screening, hiring and training professional employees, let's use the higher estimate of 2 ½ times annual pay. Now we're talking $112,500, and that's *before* we consider the costs of training, orientation, familiarity with the company's policies and customers, and so on.

Every time you lose an employee you lose some of the company's knowledge of policies and work practices. New employees make mistakes and create quality problems until they are fully trained. The time you spend training new employees takes you or one of your staff away from your regular duties, causing your work to suffer or forcing you to work longer hours. You may have to pay other employees overtime to offset lower productivity while the new employee is getting up to speed. You may also lose some continuity and credibility with your customers and suppliers, especially if they begin to believe you have a revolving door. Stability is important both from a cost reduction and a customer credibility standpoint.

Companies that enjoy lower employee turnover also have lower than average rates of employee theft and pilfering, accidents and injuries. The U.S. Chamber of Commerce estimates that dishonesty by employees costs one to two percent (1% to 2%) of gross sales each year. The Small business Administration estimates that thirty percent (30%) of business failures are directly related to employee theft.

High turnover may also be a symptom of deeper problems in the organization—poor supervision, poor training, lack of technical support, low pay, inadequate benefits, poor working conditions or a long list of other problems. And while a good system for hiring employees will not solve the myriad of other organizational problems, it will at least help you reduce new hire turnover, and that is one step in the right direction.

Where turnover is low, morale is higher, and high morale can also be tied to higher productivity. Current employees do not enjoy having to train and re-train new employees. They do not like being forced to correct their errors. They hate the problems caused by a revolving door and are much happier when the workforce is stable.

Finally, consider your own peace of mind. Whether you are managing your own business, or managing a department or company for someone else, it is impossible for you to feel good about the business when high turnover is wrecking your profits, creating customer problems and sabotaging your sales.

Hiring Right presents easy to use, straightforward techniques—**A Business Blueprint™**—you can use immediately to reduce your new hire turnover. First, you will learn what to do, <u>before</u> you start recruiting, to make sure you do not waste your time and money going in the wrong direction.

Next, you will learn some recruiting techniques that really work, at a cost you can afford. You will also learn how to screen applicants so that you interview only the best candidates.

You will learn how to conduct a valid pre-employment interview that will help you determine whether applicants *really can do* what they say they can do, and that will help you eliminate candidates who have lied or in some way "enhanced" their application or resume.

Finally, you will learn how to check references to verify what you have learned about applicants, and see some tips and guidelines for making attractive job offers.

In Part Two, there are complete, step-by-step hiring blueprints for five of the most common types of jobs: sales, entry level labor, clerical/administrative, technical, and management. Using these blueprints you can immediately begin using the new skills you learned in Part One.

And last, you'll find a discussion and some tips for avoiding legal problems in hiring; and scattered throughout the book are samples of forms you can adapt for your own use.

Architects and contractors use blueprints to plan their construction projects. The blueprint tells them what materials they need, where to put the foundation, how high to build the walls, and what quality standards they must meet each step of the way. It would be impossible to build a quality home without these instructions.

This book is your blueprint for reducing new hire turnover and increasing your profits. Let's get started!

Part One
A Business Blueprint™ for Basic Hiring Skills

Chapter One: Develop a Profile of the "Ideal" Employee

Before you begin recruiting to fill your open positions, you should first develop a "profile" of the ideal employees for each position. There are several methods presented here, and even though it is tempting to skip this step, please don't. You may believe it is not necessary, or takes too much time, or is too complicated. After all, you already know everything you need to know about your jobs, right?

Wrong. If you skip this step, you might make one of these common hiring mistakes.

Mistake Number One

The first mistake is assuming a level of education, experience or skill that is not really necessary to perform the job. That will limit your applicant pool and cause your hiring process to be too long, expensive and frustrating.

For example, say you are going to fill the position of an entry-level bookkeeping clerk. You might assume that in order to operate a personal computer, enter receivables and payables into the accounting system and run some routine monthly reports, candidates must be high school or even college graduates.

But if you think about the skill levels required, you will realize the position does not necessarily demand a specific diploma. What it does require is good math and data entry skills, and attention to detail. It requires a basic understanding of the differences between a debit and a credit. And it requires skill in using PC-based spreadsheet programs. There are many people who have all these skills, but may not have a high school diploma or college degree.

Here is another example. A non-profit agency ran a help-wanted ad in a regional newspaper. The position was administrative assistant and required a college degree, computer word processing and spreadsheet skills, and five years' experience in an administrative or secretarial position. The pay advertised was $16,000 annually for a full time schedule. After three weeks, there were no qualified applicants.

The ad was run a second time with the same results. After six frustrating weeks with no applicants, the requirements were reduced to computer word processing and spreadsheet training, two years' experience, good verbal and written communications skills, and the desire to make a difference for the people served by this agency. The ad was run again with the new requirements, and the position was filled within a week.

The agency had made a mistake by assuming a college degree was required (the previous incumbent had a degree) when a degree was not necessary. They spent several weeks and more than two thousand dollars of unnecessary expense looking for someone they did not need. Also, the requirements placed on the job were not realistic for the pay level. In that market, administrative assistants with five years' experience and good technical skills were starting at $24,000 or more annually. It was a time consuming, costly mistake on the part of the hiring agency.

In other words, take time to think carefully about the skill, knowledge and experience requirements of the job. Consider how much time and effort you can spend training someone. Ask yourself if anyone has ever done the job successfully without the skills you are requiring? Look at the backgrounds of other successful employees in that position. Consider the pay level and your community's job market. Be realistic about the job, and you can save yourself time, money and frustration.

Mistake Number Two

The second major mistake is trying to hire someone just like you.

Josh Taylor is a master machinist who started his own company several years ago. As his reputation and the business grew, he hired other machinists to help with the workload. During the past two years, he has had an average of six employees at any given time.

Josh gained his skill by a combination of education and experience. He completed a two-year technical degree program right out of high school, then apprenticed for six years in another shop before opening his own business. Since that is the way he learned the craft, Josh assumed others would learn that way as well. He always insisted that his employees had either finished the two-year tech program, or were enrolled at the time they started to work for him. He expected they would be willing to work several years as apprentices before moving on or demanding more pay.

During the last two years, however, Josh hired a total of seventeen apprentice machinists, for a turnover rate of 35%. Every person he hired with the two-year degree left within six months, in spite of competitive wages. The four he hired who were enrolled in the tech program left within a few months after finishing the degree. The only employees who stayed a full year were those who did not finish the program for one reason or another.

On the basis of this track record, it may be a mistake for Josh to continue hiring machinists with that two-year technical school degree. As soon as they finish their school, they move on. Josh needs to realize the market has changed and adjust his hiring criteria accordingly. He might find someone with basic high school training and plenty of talent, who takes pride in seeing a finished product, and is willing to start in an entry-level position. The increased training time in that situation will more than pay for itself with lower turnover and higher morale among the workers.

Mistake Number Three

The third mistake is hiring someone you like.

We've all done it, of course. We interview several candidates, none of whom are really well qualified for our job. Frustrated, we decide we will never find the "perfect" candidate, and just hire the applicant we liked the best, the one with whom there was some charisma. "She'll be able to learn what she needs to know," we tell ourselves.

James was a good example. A tall, good-looking young man with a Tom Cruise smile, he applied for the position of safety analyst with a small manufacturing company. He interviewed with the plant manager and general manager, both of whom were impressed by his "can do" attitude. They were willing to overlook his spotty work history and the fact that he had no experience with, or interest in, industrial safety. What he wanted was a job, and he sold them on himself.

The job had originally been envisioned as a plant nurse who would administer basic first aid, deal with worker's compensation paperwork, shepherd injured workers through the rehabilitation process and back to work, and develop a safety program to reduce accidents and injuries. But after they met James, the two managers decided to re-design the job, eliminating the nursing requirements and making the position more of a professional level position. They also substantially increased the starting pay above what had been budgeted.

Within three months, James was bored and lobbying for a different job. He hated the paperwork aspects of his job and did not enjoy working with injured employees. He was not making "enough" money and wanted more. He began criticizing his supervisor and the other management staff, seizing on every opportunity to make himself look good at someone else's expense. After causing turmoil and dissention for nearly eighteen months, James' position was eliminated and his employment terminated.

In other words, developing a profile of the "ideal" candidate will give you a more objective basis for hiring, and help you prevent new-hire turnover.

Profile the Job First

There are two major reasons for profiling each job. First, if you have more than fifteen employees, your company is covered by the Americans with Disabilities Act and you are required to document the physical requirements of a job *before* you start recruiting to fill that position. The techniques you are about to learn will fulfill that requirement.

More important, completing a job profile, such as the one illustrated, will help you focus on the job in a specific way so you can find just the right person. You will think about what you need in terms of primary job duties, performance standards, skills, knowledge, experience, training, licenses and certifications. You will also think about working conditions and the physical requirements of the job. When you have completed a job profile, you will know everything you need to know about the job.

Here are some examples.

List the Primary Tasks

First, list the primary job tasks and duties—the reason the job exists. Avoid using terms like "responsible for…" Leave out information about what skills and knowledge are required; those will come later. *What is it the job actually does? What do you see people doing? What are the expected outcomes of the job?* The more specific you can be, the easier recruiting will be. Here are some partial job duties lists for three different jobs:

Press Operator Primary Job Duties:

- Set up and print newspapers on a Goss Community Press.
- Perform routine preventive maintenance on the press and related equipment.
- Operate a forklift to receive, move, load and store bulk newsprint and supplies.
- Take and report inventory of equipment and supplies.
- Keep pressroom, storage areas and break areas clean and neat.

Clerk Typist Primary Job Duties:

- Type submitted stories into the computer for editing and layout.
- Proofread and correct errors, and verify submitted information.
- Call correspondents and take information over the phone; type that material into the computer.
- Relieve switchboard operator for breaks.

Construction Helper Primary Job Duties:

- Help carpenters with general construction duties.
- Drive company truck to and from the construction sites.

- Read job orders and load correct materials and supplies onto the truck.
- Keep truck, yard and shop areas clean and neat.
- Take truck for basic maintenance as required. Keep maintenance records up to date.

In addition to these specific lists, there is also a group of duties that include the "softer" skills involved in every job. You can add this list to the end of almost any specific primary job duties list:

- Maintains close communications with supervisor and other employees. Works from either written or verbal instructions.
- Maintains a friendly, helpful attitude toward customers and co-workers.
- Meets all standards for personal conduct, appearance, safety and housekeeping.
- Actively seeks ways to improve company operations.
- Complies with all policies and procedures.

In short, when you list the primary duties of a job, think in terms of *what*, rather than how or why. Use action verbs like writes, plans, sells, cuts, lays out, operates, drives, designs, types, balances, counts, edits, proofreads, contacts, negotiates, paints, cleans. For each function you list, show what percentage of time the person will spend doing that particular function. The percentages should total close to one hundred percent (100%).

Next, list on the job profile any secondary functions of the job. These are things that might be a routine part of the job but are not the reason the job exists, and could also be done by someone else. For example, most job profiles include the phrase, "Other duties as required or assigned." That gives you the freedom to do cross training so that someone can back up another position.

A clerk typist might do routine filing as a secondary function. A bookkeeper may take turns performing the daily or weekly computer system backup. These functions are

Sample List of Action Verbs

Arrange	Solder	Calibrate	Schedule
Balance	Train	Move	Haul
Assign	Edit	Teach	Solve
Coordinate	Clean	Create	Set Up
Type	Report	Enter	Diagnose
Transcribe	Negotiate	Calculate	Manage
Copy	Direct	Program	Supervise
Write	Print	Troubleshoot	Interview
Design	Produce	Diagnose	Proofread
Distribute	Solve	Drive	Assemble
Calibrate	Plan	Estimate	Mix
Sell	Control	Test	Paint

important, but they are not *"the reason the job exists."* List any of these secondary duties.

We make the distinction between primary and secondary job duties because of the Americans with Disabilities Act. The ADA requires that companies make "reasonable accommodations" for handicapped or disabled applicants who are "otherwise qualified to perform the essential (primary) functions" of a job. Since these accommodations can end up costing you a lot of money, it is important to accurately document both the primary and secondary job functions. By doing that, you will know exactly what the job requires and can comply with the law in a positive way.

Performance Standards

Now go back to the top of the list and add the performance standards for each of the job functions you listed. Performance standards list the minimum acceptable performance for employees who are fully trained in all aspects of the job. Think of performance standards for the press operator job duties we wrote earlier.

Press Operator Job Duties

Essential Duties:

- Set up and print newspapers on a Goss Community Web press.

- Perform all duties necessary to set up, prepare and print newspapers and other printed materials as assigned.

- Follow all safety guidelines.

- Perform routine preventive maintenance on the press and related equipment.

- Operate a forklift to receive, move, load and store bulk newsprint and supplies.

- Keep pressroom, storage areas and break areas clean and neat.

- Maintain close communications with supervisor and other employees; works from either written or verbal instructions.

- Maintains a friendly, helpful attitude toward customers and co-workers.

- Meets all standards for personal conduct, appearance and housekeeping.

- Actively seeks ways to improve company operations.

- Maintains compliance with all company policies and procedures.

Press Operator Performance Standards

- Meets all approved quality standards and deadlines.

- No accidents or injuries. Achieves forklift operator's license within 30 days of employment and maintains license in active status.

- No breakdowns or lost time because of failure to maintain press and equipment.

- Follows all operating policies and procedures. No waste because of failure to follow approved procedures.

- Paperwork is properly completed and approved on a timely basis. Monthly inventory is in balance.

- People are kept informed; no surprises. Customers and supervisors report they are satisfied. No complaints or observed problems.

- Absences are limited to earned time off with pay. On time for work and breaks.

- Work and break areas are neat and clean. Wears approved uniform.

- Is cross-trained in at least one other job.

- Participates in group problem solving as needed.

- Suggests ways to improve procedures or systems.

- Meets all established standards of performance.

In addition to helping you zero in on the job, performance standards will also be used to screen applicants during the interviewing process, and to train new employees once they have been hired. Think in terms of how you will evaluate the employee's performance and be as specific as possible.

Finally, for each of the job functions, list the approximate percentage of time employees will spend doing things. Try to divide the list so that the primary functions make up about 85-90% of the time, with the remaining time allotted for secondary functions.

Knowledge, Skills, Attitudes

Now that both the primary and secondary job duties and performance standards have been documented, in the next sections of the job profile you will list the knowledge, skills, aptitudes and other characteristics that are necessary for a _new person_ to perform the _minimum requirements of the job._ Think carefully about what you really need, and avoid requiring more than is really necessary. For the clerk typist position, for example, you may want to list completion of a basic computer word processing class, and/or passing a pre-employment test, and good grammar, spelling and punctuation skills. Anything else might be more than is required for someone to perform the minimum job requirements.

An example: Requires six months' previous factory experience. Must be able to speak, read and write English with clarity and perform basic math at the 6th grade level or above. Previous experience working an evening or night shift preferred.

For the general labor position, the only education or experience required would be basic reading and math skills so the employee can read the schedule, pick up the supplies needed, perform the inventory tasks and keep the truck maintenance records. And for the press operator, you will want to require reading and math skills and previous work experience on a web press.

The key words in this section are *necessary, new person,* and *minimum requirements*. In other words, think of the amount of training you are willing to do, and start from there.

Then be specific about your equipment, systems and procedures. For example, you might need the clerk typist to have experience with a "Windows-based personal computer and operating systems, and Microsoft Word 7or higher." Your construction helper will need to drive a commercial vehicle. And your press operator will be running a Goss Community press. Since these are entry level positions, instead of requiring those skills you might want to say "helpful" or "desired." That way you can target them without needlessly limiting your applicant pool. If you don't have time to do the training, however, you will want to require that applicants already have those skills.

Now, list any other specific, technical requirements that go with the job. The construction helper, for example, must have a valid driver's license, and be able to secure a commercial operator's license within 30 days of employment.

Work Environment

Next, turn to the general work environment and list things that will affect the job in question. The construction helper will work outdoors in all kinds of weather conditions. The clerk typist will work in a crowded, noisy office where there will be lots of ringing telephones and frequent interruptions. The press operator may need to work evening hours, wear hearing protection and wear a work uniform. Some jobs require frequent overtime or split shifts. Sales jobs often require use of a personal vehicle and sometimes willingness to work weekends or evenings. Many jobs require meeting daily, weekly or monthly deadlines. Some jobs require dealing with customer complaints. Think about all the things that make up the environment where your jobs are performed and list everything. In this area it is better to list too much than to leave out something that will surprise an applicant or new employee.

For example: Factory is somewhat noisy. Safety hazards include moving equipment such as forklifts, automated equipment and a moving production line.

Personal Qualities

Now list the personal qualities you will be looking for that will help you determine whether a candidate *will do* the job and is a *fit* for your environment. You might think of this as the "personality" or "attitude" section. For example, if your job includes a requirement for meeting a daily deadline, then list that. If your administrative position requires doing work for several people and dealing with conflicting priorities, you might list those things.

Also, it is important to balance the team. For instance, if you are sales-oriented and outgoing, you might want to balance your skills with someone who is more analytical and attentive to details.

Example: Must be able to tolerate a continuously fast pace. Must be challenged by quality and productivity demands without becoming overly stressed. Must be able to work alone for extended periods, without close supervision. Must be willing to comply with all policies, procedures and standards including attendance, punctuality, productivity, safety, waste and quality. Must also be able to work as a member of a team when required.

Physical Requirements

Finally, list everything you can think of that requires physical or mental ability. For example, even the most sedentary office jobs might require standing to file, vision to use the computer, the ability to speak clearly and be understood over the telephone, and manual dexterity to handle paperwork and keyboarding. If there is lifting involved, show how much weight must be moved and how often it must be moved. List everything you can think of. A complete picture of the job is critical.

And remember that even people who are handicapped or disabled in some way may be able to do more than you think; don't eliminate candidates from consideration because of an obvious disability. Instead, after you have listed all the physical requirements of the job during an interview, *ask* the candidates "Will you be able to perform all the requirements of the job?" To make sure you're not in violation of any laws, ask the same question of *all* candidates. People may have hidden disabilities, after all. Another good question to ask *all* candidates: "Are there any accommodations we'll need to make so that you can perform all the requirements of the job?" Of course, you'll need to consider any accommodations discussed, but at this point you're not agreeing to make those accommodations. However, in my experience, accommodations made for people who are in some way disabled or handicapped also make the job easier for non-disabled employees, so please keep an open mind.

For example: Must be able to bend, reach, stoop, handle parts and hear 100% of the time. Must be able to move and lift up to 30 pounds frequently throughout the shift.

Ask for Input

As a final check to make sure you have included all the information you need to form an accurate picture of the job you are about to fill, consider talking to someone who is doing the job. They may think of something you have left out, or may have a different point of view you need to include.

Documenting your jobs in this way takes a little extra time on the front end—about thirty minutes for each job—but you will be using the job questionnaire throughout the hiring process. It will also be a basic training document. The time you spend now will be repaid many times over in the form of better hires, lower turnover, shorter training times and fewer misunderstandings about what is expected of employees. Think of it as "preventive maintenance" for employees.

Research the Job History

A second method for developing a profile of the "ideal" applicant involves reviewing the records of past employees in this job to see if you can draw some conclusions about the kind of people who leave the job and the kind who stick with it for some period of time. In some cases this will be relatively easy and the mistakes will stand out. In most situations, however, it will take a careful, in-depth analysis to answer any questions. It is a time-consuming project that is not fun, but will definitely yield dividends for your business.

For one company, a $30 million food processing company with just under 200 full-time employees, first year turnover for the entry level labor position had been running sixty-nine percent (69%), with an annual cost of $430,000. In the first year after a records analysis (job history) was done, the hiring process was changed to reflect the findings and turnover was reduced to less than twenty-six percent (26%), for a savings of $240,000. The following year saw even more savings. A manufacturing company with 165 employees and an outdoor advertising company with fewer than one hundred employees both had similar dramatic results.

This is how you do it.

Set a Time Period

First, establish a time period as a benchmark for success with new employees. For some of the more technical or highly skilled jobs, it may be several years, but for entry level positions it will likely be just one year. That should be enough time for you to train the employee, and then recoup the hiring and training costs in the form of sustained job performance that meets your production and quality standards.

So, for the press operator position we are trying to fill, we will use one year as the benchmark. In other words, employees who were hired as press operators and stayed one year or more were "good" hires. Those who left *for any reason* before their first anniversary were "bad" hires. This is a mature job, so we will look at the records on everyone who was hired or transferred into a press operator position within the past five years.

Pull Records

Pull the files of all employees who were hired into the position in question, including current employees. Divide the files into two groups:

Good Hires:
- Current employees who have been in the position for twelve months or more, along with
- Former employees whose employment was terminated or who left *for any reason AFTER twelve months*.

Bad Hires:
- Former employees whose employment was terminated or who left *for any reason BEFORE twelve months.*

How many records you will pull depends on how long the job has existed, but for a long-standing, well-established job, go for a minimum of three years' data. Five years' worth of data would be better.

Start with the Good Hires, and the current employees. Use only the data you had available when you hired them, such as their application for employment and interview notes. (Using information you have gathered about them since they have been employees, such as work records and payroll files, will distort your data, so be careful not to do that.) Enter onto a spreadsheet each item of data you can find on the employment application, test results, references checks, interview notes, and other pre-employment data. If you cannot find specific bits of data in the files, leaves those items blank, but it is important to sift through the information as carefully as possible or the analysis will not be as valuable as it could be.

Sample List of Data Needed for a Records Analysis:

Gender	Male or Female
Hiring Source	(Employee, friend, relative, news ad, agency, etc.)
Employment Status When Hired	Empl FT, Empl PT, Unemployed, Retired
If unemployed, how long	Number of months
Average Length of Previous Empl.	<6 mo., 6 mo. To 1 yr., 1-2 yrs., 2-3 yrs., etc.
Total Work Experience	Number of months
Distance from Home to Work	Number of miles
Education	<High school grad, GED, High school grad, some tech, 2-yr. degree, some college, bachelor's degree, graduate degree, other
Average Pay Rate	<$8/hr., $8-10/hr., etc.
Was position a move up	Yes No
Other data particular to your job or industry	

At this stage of the exercise, do not try to draw any conclusions; just enter the data from each file onto your analysis chart or spreadsheet.

Create Spreadsheet Formulas

Build into your spreadsheet some formulas to calculate the various bits of data. For example, one bit of data you will record is "average length of employment." This is the total length of time the applicant worked at all jobs during the previous ten year period, expressed in months, and divided by the number of jobs held. Include periods of school or unemployment and count them as if they were jobs. For example, if there were four jobs and two periods of unemployment for a total of 120 months, the average length of employment is 30 months.

For hiring source, your options include employee referrals friends, relatives, newspaper ad, temporary agency, etc. Employment status when hired includes employed full-time, employed part-time, unemployed, retired, and so on. Express lengths of time in months, such as less than six months, six months to one year, and so on. Distance from home to work is shown in miles.

Once you have the data entered for your current employees, move on to those employees who left the job after more than twelve months. Since they remained in the job more than twelve months they were "good" hires. Add their data to the current employees file.

Now turn to the "Bad Hires," the files on all the people who were hired into your job but left for any reason before their first anniversary date. Record the data as before, but keep this file separate from the "good" hires file.

It is not necessary to enter data on current employees who have been in the job less than twelve months, since you don't know yet whether they are "good" or "bad hires. If you do include these employees, however, you will soon be able to predict with remarkable accuracy which employees will eventually leave and which will stay to become long-term employees.

Analyze the Data

Finally, analyze the data and draw conclusions about your potentially "ideal" applicants. Look for indicators that will predict, based on past experience, which applicants will stay for twelve months and which applicants will leave the company during that time. And be prepared for some surprises.

One company found, for example, that its best candidates among the men were those who had completed high school plus at least one year of technical training. The best candidates among the women, however, were those who did not graduate high school but had completed their GED. Among the men, the best candidates were those who had been working full-time at another company at the time of their application. Among the women, the best candidates had been unemployed for at least six months at the time of application.

You can also use the data to develop an applicant score sheet, assigning values to each item of data according to its proven significance in your study. Then, as you review applications, you will set aside each of the candidates who are clearly outside the profile that experience has proven will produce low turnover.

Complete a Personality Profile

A third method for learning who is your "ideal candidate" involves having each applicant, or at least the final group of applicants, complete a personality profile. This is especially helpful if your employees work in a team environment or have responsibility for sales or customer service.

Study after study over the last forty years has proven the job-related validity of personality tests. We know, for example, that there are *eight major personality traits* that can be reliably predicted. We know that these personality traits will *reliably predict success in certain types of jobs*. And we know that when we *match the person to the job, we can predict both job performance and satisfaction, and ultimately, turnover.*

The Craft Personality Questionnaire (CPQ) is an example of one profile that is both inexpensive and easy to understand. It has been repeatedly validated for pre-employment screening, and compatibility charts have been developed for more than forty of the most complex jobs, including outside sales, inside sales, customer service, financial services sales, bank teller, personal banker, engineer, administrative manager and personnel clerk.

Using the CPQ as part of a three-year validation study, one bank found a strong *correlation between certain CPQ scores and turnover* for both tellers and personal bankers. There was also a *correlation between CPQ scores and successful job performance.*

In another CPQ study, an insurance company compared the validity of its biographical data as a pre-screening device, to that of the CPQ. The study compared the job performance of new hires that scored within the recommended range of the CPQ to new hires whose scores were outside the recommended range. *Those who were within the compatibility range sold an average of $88,000 per year more* *than those who were outside the compatibility range.* The total difference was $53 million dollars!

Apparently CraftSystems is no longer in business. However, The American Psychological Association should be able to help you find other vendors for personality profiles. Just be certain that their tests, or profiles, have been validated for the jobs you need to fill, or be ready to complete a validation study yourself. This requires proving to the EEOC (Equal Employment Opportunity Commission) that the tests are valid—actually test skills they claim to test—and actually test the skills that are really required by the jobs (For more information, contact the author using the information in the last page of this book.

Is This Legal?

But aren't the kinds of pre-hire techniques described illegal, you ask. Absolutely not. In fact, Federal regulations strongly encourage, and in some cases require, that job profiles be developed *before* recruiting begins. Over and over again, the Equal Employment Opportunity Commission (EEOC) and the Courts have approved pre-hire processes that were proved valid and reliable predictors of job success.

The key is that all three methods described must be proven to be representative of the jobs to be filled (valid), and reliable predictors of job success. You will only know that for sure when you have gathered data for several years, and completed a thorough analysis.

But in the meantime, get started by developing a comprehensive profile of the "ideal" candidate. And include your current recruiting as part of your validation study, with a statement to that effect on the Application for Employment.

To summarize, turnover is expensive. In some cases, it costs businesses tens of thousands of dollars a year in lost productivity, administrative costs, loss of business, poor quality and a host of other direct and indirect expenses. Making a poor job match during the hiring process is a sure route to turnover, but using the methods presented to find an "ideal" candidate profile, you can make major improvements in your turnover numbers and the associated costs.

And, although the methods presented for doing this validation do take a little extra time and require some discipline on your part, the resulting payoff is fast and goes directly to the bottom line. Besides, they've all been validated by the EEOC as solid predictors of job success. What's not to like about that?

Chapter Two: Recruiting and Screening Applicants

Once you are clear about the job and the person you need to hire, you can begin the recruiting process. You may find that some recruiting techniques work better during periods of high unemployment while other techniques work better when the economy is good and unemployment is low. Some techniques will work better in small communities and others will work better in larger cities. You will learn through experience what works best for you.

There is a general "rule of thumb," however: you should *always use more than one recruiting method*. Using a combination of methods helps get the word out to a diverse group of applicants and gives you a better chance of finding the best person for the job. Limiting yourself to only one or two methods will unnecessarily limit your hiring choices, and may lead to charges of discrimination.

Promotion from Within

When faced with a vacancy in your company or department, the first place to look for applicants is among your current employees. Promoting from within is the least costly recruiting method. It gives you the advantage of knowing the current job performance of applicants. Internal promotion and transfer also helps develop high morale and reduce turnover as employees realize there is potential for growth and advancement.

You will have reduced training times when you promote employees who already know something about the company and the job. There will be fewer quality problems with people whose work you have seen. Your company will develop a better reputation with your customers and in the community as a good place to work. And you will incur fewer administrative costs associated with, reference checking and employee benefits changes.

A tremendous payoff also comes in the form of greater employee loyalty and willingness to extend extra effort for you and the company. When people see that they have a career path, and that you have confidence in their ability to do more, they will knock themselves out for you.

To make sure internal applicants understand the job for which they are applying, give them a copy of the job profile and performance standards you developed, and any additional information you have about the job. This will make recruiting much easier and help reduce confusion and misunderstanding about what the job involves. Make it clear to all internal applicants that the final hiring decision is up to you. No one is a "shoo-in" for the job. Everyone has to qualify, and the final decision will be based on qualifications, not seniority or time in grade or who the applicant knows.

When you do promote someone from within, you may create a domino effect of other promotions and transfers. While that will initially create some confusion and inefficiencies, it is still less expensive than recruiting from outside your company. The position you will ultimately fill from outside will be a more entry level position that costs less to fill, and that cost will be offset by the advantages of using people you know.

Employee Referrals

Another inexpensive recruiting method is employee referrals. At the same time you are letting employees know of internal career opportunities, you can also ask them to refer their friends and acquaintances who might be qualified for the position. Because of potential discrimination issues, this method should *always* be used in tandem with at least one other recruiting method.

In addition to lower recruiting costs, employee referrals have another advantage. Several long-term studies of employee turnover have found that *the lowest new-hire turnover occurs among people who were hired through employee referrals.* There may be several reasons:

- Applicants may be hearing from your employees that your company is a "good place to work." That counts for a lot.
- Second, it is easier for people to make a job change if they already know someone at the new company and are not walking in cold.

- Finally, employees are hesitant to refer people who are not qualified, for fear they will be embarrassed by the referral's poor job performance. They also will not refer people they are not willing to work with, so they will try to eliminate people who are unreliable or hard to get along with.

If the principle of low turnover for employee referrals holds true for you, it will mean lower overhead costs and potentially higher profits.

Accepting employee referrals will be easier for you if you follow a few simple guidelines.

- First, make sure employees understand they should make no promises or commitments to potential applicants.

- Employees should limit their discussion of the job and leave it up to you to talk about qualifications, pay, working conditions and other aspects of the job.

- Employees should encourage their acquaintances to come in to the office to apply, or to apply on-line, if that option is available, but should never be allowed to take applications out of the office for someone to fill out elsewhere.

- Limit the employee's involvement to making the initial contact and leave the rest up to you.

And here is something else to consider. During periods of very low unemployment when there are more jobs open than there are qualified applicants to fill them, you might benefit from offering a hiring bonus to employees who successfully refer applicants. Structure the bonus so it is paid in installments: $50 upon application, $50 upon hire, $100 after completing ninety days, as an example. Vary the amounts according to the job market and the job level. Bonuses like this will not only generate more qualified applicants, they will also give the referring employee a vested interest in helping the new employee get off to a good start. In some situations, you might also need to pay the same bonus to the new employee as an extra incentive.

Hiring relatives

Some companies also take the employee referral process a step further and hire relatives of current employees. There are both positive and negative arguments concerning hiring of relatives.

On the plus side, it's an easy, inexpensive way to recruit, especially for positions like summer vacation replacements, temporary jobs or part-time positions. Employees who have children in college will be truly grateful for the extra money a child can earn through a summer job.

On the negative side, if a relative does not work out for some reason, you will have two unhappy employees. Spouses have been known to divorce, and when that happens while both are employed at the same company, the process can be disastrous for everyone concerned. Parents have no objectivity when it comes to the job performance of their children and have been known to create real problems for supervisors who are just trying to do their job.

If you do decide to take advantage of employee referrals for relatives, consider limiting their hiring to temporary or part-time positions. Make sure the relatives work in different departments. And under no circumstances should you ever allow an employee to supervise a relative.

Make sure employees understand that you will be the judge of who is qualified or not qualified, and that the hiring decision is yours. An employee referral may help an applicant get a foot in the door but is no guarantee of a job. Once the referral is made, the employee should bow out and leave the process and the decision up to you.

When you do accept employee referrals, it is important to treat them exactly as you treat all other applicants. Fairness, and the perception of fairness, is important. If outside applicants feel they were locked out without fair consideration, you may have to deal with time-consuming complaints, unhappy customers or vendors, or a formal investigation. Prevent these problems by giving all applicants full consideration.

Networking

Each of us has a network of friends, family, professional associates, vendors and suppliers, neighbors, fellow club members, church friends and others we are in contact with from time to time. When you have a job opening to fill, tap into that network for qualified referrals. It is estimated that most people can list up to 250 people they know at a given time. These contacts can be a low cost source of qualified applicants if you know how to work with them.

Obviously, you don't want to contact every single acquaintance every time you have a job open. Be selective to avoid overkill. If you "go to the well" too often you will eventually find the well dry.

If you are looking for management and professional level applicants, contact only the people on your networking list who are likely to have contact with those applicants. Other professionals like insurance and real estate agents, professional association members and your contacts at non-competing companies may be able to refer other professional applicants. On the other hand, your landscaping contractor, janitorial contractor and other vendors and suppliers who know your business may be able to refer people for your more entry level positions.

Again, be careful to follow your complete hiring process with network-referred applicants to avoid the appearance of favoritism or discrimination.

Applications on File

Remember to look through your active applications file to see if a qualified person has already applied. By law, all applications must be kept on file for twelve months; in some states the requirement is 24 months. Most companies keep applications "active" for thirty days. If your position is entry level or you have recently filled another similar position, you may find a candidate in this file. If your position requires specific technical skills or background, or if it has been a long time since you filled a similar position, there will likely *not* be an available candidate here.

Newspaper Ads

One of the most frequently used recruiting methods is placing a "help wanted" ad in the newspaper. This is an excellent resource for many positions and is usually cost effective. Here are some things to remember when you place help-wanted advertising:

- Be specific enough in listing the job requirements so that only qualified applicants will respond. The ad should both attract and qualify potential applicants.

- Give as many details as possible related to working conditions. List most or all the factors you listed on the job profile.

- Unless you are in an unusual competitive situation, listing the starting pay will help eliminate some curiosity seekers or those who are overqualified for the position, especially for entry level positions.

- Be sure to include specific information about when and how to apply.

- Highlight the advantages of working for your company. "Sell" both the company and the career opportunity. Many people who are not actively looking for a job regularly read the help-wanted advertising. Over time, these ads reinforce your company as a good place to work and enhance your image in the community. Sell, sell, sell.

- Remember that all help-wanted advertising must solicit applications *without* regard to gender, age, race, religious background, color, national origin, handicap or veteran status. Ads should be placed by job category, such as "clerical" or "general help wanted," and should never include references that could be found to be discriminatory. References to age, gender, marital status, appearance or other personal characteristics must never be included in a help-wanted ad. Each ad should include the phrase "Equal Opportunity Employer."

When it comes to writing newspaper ads, you will need to experiment to learn what works best in your market and for a particular job. There are some basic guidelines, however:

- White space sells. Whether you place your ad "in-column" or as a "display," let the person taking the ad know you want plenty of white space at the top and bottom of the ad. Paying for two lines of white space at the top and two lines at the bottom will substantially increase your readership. For display ads, buy enough space to allow white space on all four sides of the type.

- Different is good. Look at the classified section in which your ad will be appearing. Study the ads, then think of some way to present your job that is different from all the others. If your company has a unique logo, use it. If everyone else in your job category is doing in-column ads, try doing a display. Borders and boxes also help separate your ad from the others.

- Use strong words. Most classified ads use the job title as the headline, but headlines work in classified advertising just as they do in the news section. Also, you need to sell your job and the headline is a good place to start. For many of your entry level positions, try "Job Hunting?" or "Looking for a Better Job?" or "Move Up to a Better Job." These phrases are proven winners and will pull more applicants, and better qualified applicants, than headings such as "Factory" or "Clerical."

- Consider the job. One company had an opening for a Division Secretary. The position had been advertised for several weeks but the people who were applying did not have the levels of skill and experience the job required. The headline on the ad was changed from "Division Secretary" to "Professional Secretary." Nothing else in the ad was changed, but the next day six well-qualified applicants inquired about the job, and one was hired before the end of the week. One word can make a tremendous difference, so it is important to understand the job and use that understanding to build an ad that will pull qualified applicants.

- Again, sell your company. In many cases, your best applicants will be those who are still working for another company. To get them to move, you need to convince them the situation at your company is better for them than the situation at their current company. Higher pay, better benefits, daytime hours, lots of overtime, no overtime, better working conditions and a chance to move up are among the things applicants look for in a better job. If you can offer those things, plug them in your ads. For example, a manufacturing company touted its "air-conditioned plant" and successfully attracted dozens of qualified, experienced applicants who were tired of working in sweat-shop conditions at other plants.

- Variety is important. Studies have shown sixty percent (60%) of an ad's response will come the first week it is run. That drops to 30% and 10% the second and third weeks. Even your best ads will not be effective forever. Change your ads each week and save the best draws for the most important jobs.

- Timing is everything. Even the best ads will not pull on a holiday week-end, so don't waste your money. In most markets, Sunday is the best day for help-wanted advertising. Wednesday runs a poor second. Other days are a waste of money.

- Always review and approve a proof copy of newspaper ads before they actually run. It does no good to get a price adjustment or refund on an ad with errors if those errors cost you valuable time and applicant confusion. No matter how good the classified ad staff at your newspaper is, remember that even the best people can make an occasional error. Be sure those errors don't happen in your classified ad!

Sample In-Column Ad:

Jump Start Your Career
Let us pay for your College degree!

Burger Bar is now hiring Counter staff for all shifts. We can work around your Class schedule. Starting pay$8 per hour with minimum guarantee. Apply in person at . . .
    Equal Opportunity Employer

Sample Display Ad:

Jump Start Your CAREER!

Let us pay for your college degree!

Burger Bar is now hiring counter staff for all shifts. We can work around your class schedule. Starting pay $8/hour with minimum guarantee. Move up based on your job performance. Paid medical and free tuition after one year! Apply in person at

Equal Opportunity Employer

Trade Publications

    Like newspapers, trade publications can be an excellent source of applicants. Jobs that require a particular technical expertise, like engineering or management-level positions, are well suited to trade publication advertising. Local chapter newsletters, regional or national newsletters and magazines are all possibilities.

    As a general rule, trade publications will cost more than newspapers for the same ad, and because of a limited publication schedule, the length of time between placing an ad and receiving responses can be several weeks or even months. Even with those limitations, however, trade publications are still a good resource. Your ad will be seen by people who have the qualifications you need. Qualified people who are not actively looking for a job may see your ad and call it to the attention of someone who is looking. And again, applicants who come to you from these sources usually meet your technical qualifications.

While you are placing an ad in trade publications, make sure you request that local and regional trade associations "post" your opening at their meetings or in their placement service. Many technical jobs are filled without an ad ever being run.

Before you decide to run ads in any national publication, whether it is a trade publication or a newspaper, make sure you are willing to pay travel expenses for candidates to come for interviews, and for people you hire to relocate. If you're not willing to pay those interviewing and relocation expenses, you're wasting your money with national ads.

The Internet

If you have decided to advertise nationally, an effective source is the Internet. If you have a Web page, list your job openings with full descriptions and a hot link to application and contact information. If you don't have a Web page, you can list your jobs on someone else's Web page for a nominal fee. Monster.com and CareerBuilder.com are two of the most popular sites, and don't forget the Web sites of your professional associations.

Any Internet advertising is competing for attention with tens of thousands of other Web sites and links, so it is especially important to write good copy and present the ad in an attractive, eye-catching way. Unless you're a trained copy writer, you may want to invest a few dollars in having a professional develop your Internet copy and links for you.

And keep in mind the Internet is a medium of instant communications, so your response from applicants who find you that way will likely be very fast and they will expect to communicate with you through E-mail or at least a FAX number. Hot links are essential and all contacts must be followed up immediately or you will be wasting your money. Speed and accessibility are both required.

Schools and Colleges

Schools and colleges can be a valuable source of applicants, especially for entry-level technical jobs, co-operative or intern programs. Most schools have career days, intern programs, work study and other forms of school-to-work programs. Spend time developing contacts with the instructors in your specialty field so they will think of you when they have students about to graduate. Volunteer to make class presentations. Serve on an advisory board.

Many schools, colleges and trade schools solicit on-campus recruiting by companies like yours. The key to successful recruiting on school and college campuses, however, is developing a one-on- relationship with the instructors in your technical field. This will be a wise investment that will pay dividends for many years.

It's not necessary to have an active opening to participate in a job fair, but keep in mind that applicants expect to fill out applications, and will be really frustrated if you say, "I'm sorry, we don't have any openings right now but we'd be glad to hear from you when we do have an opening!" Word gets around quickly, and a year's worth of hard work will be blown in a few minutes if you're not careful. Talk to your campus contacts before you sign up for a job fair and give them a chance to tell you, "We'll catch you next time."

Employment Agencies

There are several kinds of employment agencies available to help you fill job openings. They fall into two basic categories: those that charge a fee for services, and those whose fees and expenses are paid by a governmental or nonprofit agency.

"Free" Services

The agencies whose fees are paid by a governmental or nonprofit agency include the state employment service, or "unemployment office." In some states this agency is called the Employment Security Division or Job Service.

When you list job openings with the state employment service, they will refer candidates who have applied for unemployment benefits or who are listed in the agency's files. To use the state service effectively, you must be very specific about the qualifications you need, or you will be forced to waste your time with people who don't even come close to being qualified. Consider requiring the agency to call ahead for an appointment time before sending an applicant to you. Failure to do this will result in a parade of applicants who may not meet your needs but will disrupt your day and cause frustration for everyone.

The state service will also advertise job openings for you if you're specific in your requirements and they have no qualified applicants. Many times these agencies are funded based on the number of jobs they help fill, so use that to your advantage when you have an opening. Talk with your agency representative about the kind of recruiting they will do for you, if any. If they have no plans to run an ad, you may be able to talk them into doing that, at their expense. If you need an ad and the agency is not willing to pay for it, at least use the agency's telephone number and location, and instructions to apply through the agency. Then make sure the agency really screens the candidates before they refer them to you. This is especially true during periods of high unemployment, when a single "help wanted" ad can generate several hundred applications.

Other nonprofit agencies that charge no placement fee include veteran's groups, sheltered workshops for mentally or physically handicapped members, area agencies on aging and charities such as the Salvation Army or homeless shelters. Most of these groups are prevented by their charter from accepting fees, although they can accept donations. If your positions are entry level or can use people with special needs, they can be a great recruiting resource. Some minority and women's groups may also be included in this general category.

When you work with this type of agency for recruiting, be sure you're willing to accept that many of the candidates will have special needs. For example, they may not have reliable transportation. They may not have a home and may use the agency's address and telephone number. They may have very poor work histories, or have drug or alcohol dependencies, or psychological disorders such as PTSD. If you're not willing to work with employees with these limitations, don't use these nonprofit agencies for recruiting. You'll be wasting money and creating frustration for yourself, the agency and the applicants.

If you do decide to work with a nonprofit agency, the most important thing you must do is be very specific about the qualifications of the candidates you need. Otherwise, unqualified people will be referred and you'll again be wasting money and creating frustration.

Agencies that Charge Fees

Agencies that charge a fee for service include temporary agencies, private employment agencies, executive search firms and management recruiters. In many cases, these terms are used interchangeably.

Employment agencies charge a fee based on a percentage of the employee's earnings. Twenty to 50 percent is common, depending on the level of the position. In other words, if you estimate that the weekly earnings for your new mechanic will be $400, and the agency charges you a 40% fee, your weekly cost will be $560 per week for a specified number of weeks. The fee will be payable at a specific time, such as thirty days following the placement or on the new employee's start date.

Sometimes, when working with companies that are not willing to pay a fee, agencies require the applicant to pay the fee through a weekly or monthly payment plan after they accept a job. It is *never* a good idea to allow or require an employee to pay a fee for working for you. That will inevitably lead to dissatisfaction, low morale and early turnover. If you decide to use a fee-based agency, you should *always* pay any fees involved.

One way to ease the financial burden of an employment fee is by working with a temporary agency. There are several advantages here. First, you have a chance to evaluate an applicant's job performance before you make an offer of employment. Second, it may be the fastest way to fill a position. Third, it spreads the cost of the fee over several weeks or months.

For example, if a temporary agency charges a fee of 45 percent (30 percent placement fee plus 15 percent payroll costs), that fee is added to the weekly payroll billing. If the mechanic is being paid $10 per hour, you will be billed $14.50 per hour. You will normally have to agree to retain the worker on a temporary basis for a minimum number of hours so the agency can recover their advertising and payroll costs. Once that obligation is complete, you can bring the worker onto your payroll with no further fee.

When you work with a temporary agency, the employee is the agency's, not yours. That reduces your worker's compensation and payroll tax liability for the duration of the relationship, and delays the employee's eligibility for benefits until they come onto your payroll and meet your waiting period requirements. These reductions, of course, are offset by the higher hourly rate you pay the temporary agency for the worker.

When you are working with a temporary agency, remember you are paying their fee so they should fill the job to your specifications. You should require the agency to do the advertising and screening, and refer to you only those candidates who meet your specific criteria. You should interview all final candidates before a selection is made. Be sure the agency does a background and reference check and a ten panel drug test. In other words, all aspects of the pre-employment process should be fulfilled by the temporary agency. No shortcuts should be taken.

Once a temporary worker is on board, maintain close communications with the agency representative to make sure the worker is meeting your needs. If problems develop or the worker cannot perform the minimum requirements of the job, instruct the agency to replace the worker with someone else. You should not settle for less than satisfactory job performance from your own employees, or from temporary workers. If you have already paid the agency's fee, then when the employee is replaced you should not pay the fee again.

Employment agencies that work on a "pay when hired" basis are called "contingency" firms. If they do not fill the position, they do not get paid, so that is an advantage for you. You may want to place your job order with several of these agencies at the same time, especially if you are pressed for time. If you do list with several agencies at the same time, however, be prepared for lots of phone calls from the recruiters.

Some contingency firms will want to work on an "exclusive" basis. That means you would not place the job order with anyone else. If you have a great deal of confidence in the recruiter, giving an exclusive—say, for the first thirty days—will save you some time and likely also get you the best quality applicants. On the other hand, if your recruiter is new in the business and has not developed a large network of contacts, or is not willing to advertise your position, an exclusive will only limit your applicants and extend your search time.

Before you give an agency an exclusive, work with them on several openings so you know whether they will be able to meet your needs. Talk with some of their other clients to see how they handle exclusives, and what kind of record they have. And make sure you are comfortable that the recruiter knows as much as possible about the job being filled. It does you no good to give a recruiter an exclusive, then hold back information you think is too confidential. If you trust the recruiter enough to give an exclusive, you need to be open and candid with your information.

However you choose to work with the agencies, make sure you get full service for the fee you will pay. Set some ground rules:

- Make the agency do some preliminary testing based on the job requirements. Approve the tests in advance, as well as the scoring criteria. Be sure the tests scores are not the only qualification used.

- Insist that the agency talk with you about applicants before they send them over to see you. That way you can minimize disruptions by grouping the applicants during a specific time of the day.

- Give the agency some of your applications, and make them have the applicants complete them in advance, or require on-line applications.

- Refuse to see anyone without an appointment.

- Limit the telephone calls to two or three times a day, at specified times.

Some agencies will resent working with you in this way. You should insist, however. It is your time, and it is your profits paying the bill. If they do not want to work your way, move on; there are lots of others out there who will.

Executive Search Firms

Executive search firms are at the top of the employment agency field. Some firms that call themselves executive search firms are really employment or personnel agencies working with a higher level of applicant. They accept assignments on a contingency basis, and sometimes actively market candidates to you whether you have listed a job with them or not. These firms can be very effective at finding employees in the $30,000 to $70,000 range. Above that level, select your recruiter very carefully. You will pay a substantial fee, perhaps as much as 60-to 75% of the first year salary and bonuses. And for a true executive recruiter, you'll pay the fee *in advance* of the search, and whether or not the position is filled.

For that kind of fee, you must make sure the agency is working on your behalf. Again, set some guidelines:

- Insist on seeing a resume or application before setting up an interview appointment.

- Do a telephone interview before scheduling on-site meetings. At this level, an interview may take several hours, so you don't want to see people who are not qualified.

- Make sure the agency representative, or recruiter, has done some preliminary reference checking before you see the candidate.

- And before you pay to have someone from out of town come in for an interview, do an extensive telephone interview yourself and make sure the recruiter has "qualified" the applicant's family for relocation.

Remember, your time is money. Do not waste it by doing work you are paying the recruiter to do.

Finally, be prepared for all the guidelines in this chapter to change, depending on economic conditions like the unemployment rate and so on. This is an area that is constantly in a state of flux, so keep up by reading plenty of newspapers and professional journals, talking with your professional contacts, and generally keeping your eyes open. Don't go blind into the hiring process.

If you cannot find a local candidate who suits you, *and* if you are willing to pay relocation expenses for a new employee from out of town, you may want to place your job order with one of the national agencies, such as Kelly Services, Executive Recruiters, Snelling and Snelling, or Robert Half. These franchised operations usually have a broader database, and they may ask recruiters in several parts of the country to work on your position at the same time. Again, save yourself time. Work only through your recruiter, or you will be on the phone all day with recruiters from all over the country.

Keep in mind this critical difference between contingency and retained search firms. Because they cannot be guaranteed the fee, contingency firms cannot travel to see candidates before they send them to you. They must rely on telephone interviews and reference checks. As a result, you may pay expenses for someone to come interview who is completely unsuitable because of appearance, dress, personal mannerisms and so on. It does not happen very often, but it happens to almost everyone at least once.

Retained search firms, on the other hand, charge you a substantial minimum fee, plus expenses. And they will have you sign a contract agreeing to pay the fee, or part of the fee, whether you hire their candidate or not. That means, of course, that you don't want to contract with a retained fee firm if you think Uncle Joe's next door neighbor might work out. Such contracts will include an estimate of the time it will take to fill the position, perhaps two to six months. They also include a written guarantee that if the new employee does not work out within a certain time up to a year, the firm will then fill the position for you again for no additional fee, charging only expenses.

Why use a retained fee firm at all? For positions at the executive level, a retained firm can save you tremendous time, money and headaches. At that level especially, you do not take your investment in a new employee lightly. You owe it to yourself to find the very best. You may be able to do that without retained assistance, but you may also need their help.

One of the best reasons to use a retained firm is confidentiality. If for some reason you don't want your current employees and customers to know about the opening, this is the best way to go. Retained search firms will not present candidates to you until they have personally seen several candidates, and can present only the top two or three to you. They will give you a six-or-eight page dossier on each candidate and that person's match for your position and company. You will have an opportunity to review this material in depth and talk with the recruiter about each candidate before you decide whom to interview. Only then are you asked to schedule an interview. Very expensive, but very worthwhile under certain circumstances.

If you are not accustomed to recruiting, the task can seem overwhelming. Remember to start with the job profile and target your job search for maximum benefit. Contact the recruiting sources that work best for you, always using at least two different sources for each job opening. Make sure your advertising and recruiting methods meet non-discrimination guidelines. Maintain long-term, ongoing relationships with schools and colleges. Use employment agencies when you need them, but make sure fee-payment policies are spelled out well in advance to avoid misunderstanding.

Taking and Screening Applications

At most companies, taking and screening employment applications is done by the Human Resources or Office Manager, but there may be times when the Hiring Manager will need to handle those tasks. Your goal is to find the best qualified applicants, but you must also be aware of legal issues involved in this part of the process. Careful attention to detail now helps prevent future problems.

First, consider accepting applications for employment *only when there is a job open*. By doing this, your applicant pool will be limited to a small group of people who were available at the time the job was advertised. People who apply will be qualified, interested in the job and available for work. If you accept applications at times when you have no openings, you will have an artificially inflated pool of people who were simply "putting in an application," whether or not they were qualified for a particular position.

Also, allowing people to fill out an application even when you have no job opening may result in misunderstandings and hard feelings. It is better to say, "Thanks very much for your interest, but we don't have any openings right now. We always advertise when we do have openings, and we'll be happy to have your application at that time."

On the other hand, if you are faced with filling positions where there is frequent turnover and you know it is only a matter of days before you have another opening, it may be to your advantage to accept applications *for that position* at all times. If you decide to do that, remember that you will have people apply who are neither qualified for nor interested in that position. In many cases, they will only be trying to meet the requirements for continuing to receive unemployment benefits.

Federal law requires that employment applications be kept on file for one year from the date of completion, and in some states they must be kept even longer. In addition, it is generally a good idea to list all applications received on an applicant flow log. Keeping this log will help you respond to any complaints of unfair hiring practices and is a fast reference when applicants call to check on the status of their application. And, if you are required to produce an Affirmative Action Plan each year, an applicant flow log is a required part of that Plan.

Before you consider someone an applicant, they must fill out and sign one of your company's Application for Employment forms. You may use a standard form, create your own form, or use the sample form shown in this book. There are several important elements to an employment application, and each is a critical part of the screening process. At a minimum, the Application form must include a ten-year job history, education and skills data, and contact information. Most important, it must include a place for the applicant's signature and certification of understanding.

Applicants should be certifying four important statements when they sign this form. They should be saying they understanding they will have to *pass a drug test*. They should give you *permission and a release from liability* to check their background and references. They should acknowledge the policy of *at-will employment* or the union contract, if any. They should certify that *they are who they claim to be, and are legally eligible* to work in this country. And finally, they are affirming that the *information on the application is true and complete*.

Here is an example of one company's statement at the end of the application for employment:

(Company Name) is an equal opportunity employer and does not discriminate against any applicant or employee because of race, color, religion, national origin, sex, age or disability.

"I understand that passing a pre-employment drug test is a requirement for all positions within this company. I also understand that continued compliance with the Drug and Alcohol Policy is a condition of continued employment.

"I authorize the company to conduct any necessary and reasonable investigation in connection with my application for employment, including a credit report, civil and criminal court records check, and an investigative consumer report concerning my character, general reputation, personal characteristics and mode of living. I release this company, my former employers and references from any liability or damage caused by giving and receiving information or opinions as to my employment or character.

"I understand that if my employment requires driving a vehicle, my driving record may be checked, and if it is unacceptable to the company I will not be eligible for employment; and, if employed, my failure to maintain an acceptable driving record may result in termination of my employment.

"I understand that my employment may be terminated with or without cause, and with or without notice, at any time, and that the at-will nature of my employment may not be changed or altered except by a written agreement signed by me, and by the president or chief executive officer of the company.

"I certify that I am the person I am claiming to be. I certify that I am legally eligible to work in this country. I certify that I completed and signed this application without assistance, (except in the case of a disability) and that the statements on this application are true. I understand that, if employed, any false statements or answers given or any failure to completely and fully answer any questions will be grounds for dismissal from employment."

And for companies using an electronic application process:

"I understand that my signature on this electronic application has the same force and effect as a hand-written signature."

Since an application must be filled out and signed before someone is considered an applicant, unsolicited resumes are not considered applications and are not listed on the applicant log.

Applications should be filled out by the applicant, in person, in the company's office. This is one way you can be sure applicants fill out and sign their own paperwork rather than having someone else do it for them. It is a way to make certain the applicant can read, write and follow instructions. And it avoids later problems if a question of falsification of an application should come up.

That means you should not mail applications to potential candidates or allow employees to carry an application to someone else. Have them come into the office. Candidates who have mailed a resume should fill out an application when they come in for an on-site interview. When you give someone an application, be sure they remain in the office to fill it out, then notice whether someone else helps them with the application. Never let them walk out the door with the application.

One exception to these guidelines is necessary for candidates who are recruited from out of town by you or through an agency. Because of the travel expense involved, the recruiter should give the candidate an application to complete, and that application should be part of the package you review before you authorize paying travel expense.

If you have an on-line application process, which most companies of any size now do, be sure your application has a way for candidates to attach their resume, and make sure that at some point early in the process you, or someone you trust, verifies in person that all applicants prove they are who they say they are, and certify that they filled out their own application.

"Is all this really necessary?" you ask. Absolutely. Human Resources managers have dozens of stories of their experiences with falsification of applications. Applicants who never learned to read, write and do basic math have someone else complete their application paperwork, including the screening tests. In at least one instance, a "professional" made a very good living by completing applications, taking drug tests, and sometimes even interviewing for, candidates who were unable to complete the paperwork and interview process.

Yes, of course you should make an exception for a candidate who is physically unable to complete the application process. The law requires that you make accommodations for handicapped and disabled applicants. However, if the job requires certain physical abilities, such as driving a forklift, and your candidate is blind, there may be no way to accommodate that disability.

Never assume a qualified candidate cannot perform the physical requirements. Instead, explain *in person* to that applicant the physical requirements, and say, "Would you like to take a look and explain what we can do to accommodate your disability?" If the response is 'yes,' schedule another meeting at a time when most of your employees will not be present and you can work with the applicant without a large audience present. Allow the candidate to bring a friend or relative for support, and you should also be sure you have someone present whom you trust. After the meeting, you'll need to write a brief statement explaining what happened, and the results, and have the applicant and his or her friend sign the statement. You and your friend will also sign the statement, and you will include the statement in the applicant file with the application for employment.

If all this seems like a lot of wasted time and effort, think of it this way: an hour spent now may very well eliminate an EEOC investigation down the road. And believe me, you do *not* want an EEOC investigation. If you can fax to the investigating officer copies of the application and the statement the candidate signed, you may very well avoid an on-site audit.

There is nothing wrong with an on-site audit itself, especially if you have carefully avoided any violation of Equal Opportunity guidelines. The problem is that an on-site audit opens up every avenue of investigation. The investigating officer will review all your applicant files, including those for positions other than the one at question. Your employees may be interviewed, especially the minority, female and handicapped employees. Unsuccessful applicants will be contacted and interviewed. Do you know what they will have to say about your hiring process?

Other than an interview appointment date and time, do not write anything on a candidate's application. Notes you make here may be subject to misinterpretation by someone else and could result in legal issues months, or even years later. For example, companies have been found guilty of discrimination because applications were coded to indicate appearance. There is no way you will remember, or be able to defend two years later, what your intent was when you wrote a note on an application. It is best not to write anything at all.

Taking Applications Electronically

Most companies of any size are now accepting applications electronically, using one of the Internet-based software programs available to people with access to a computer, to by-pass the traditional paper process.

If your company has a Web site, if you do business in more than one city, or if you have a high volume of applications, there are real advantages to taking electronic applications.

- The quality of your applications will immediately increase. Computer-based application software usually has built-in tools you can use to screen out less qualified, or unqualified, applicants. Those who do get through the process will meet your basic requirements.

- You will reduce your paperwork and paper storage requirements. It takes much less computer space to store electronic applications than it does to store the equivalent number of paper applications.

- Your Affirmative Action Plan applicant flow data can be pulled from your application software, saving countless hours of clerical time that is required with a manual process.

- You will get more applicants who are still working full-time when they apply for a position with you. Remember, applicants who are still working full-time elsewhere tend to have lower turnover than those who were unemployed when they applied.

- An electronic application process is more convenient if you operate in several locations. Applicants don't have to travel to make application.

- Carefully prepared and presented, an electronic application process can help prevent claims of discrimination or favoritism in the hiring process. Your process will be more consistent, and more easily controlled, than a paper process.

- If you are audited by the EEOC, some electronic processes guarantee the accuracy of the data collected and will provide the reports required for the audit. They will be your partner in preparation of your Affirmative Action Plan, if required.

- An electronic application process will reduce the time it takes to hire new employees. You will dramatically reduce the time it takes to receive and review applications. Your hiring managers can be given access to the system so they can receive applications for their open positions, eliminating the need to mail applications from one location to another.

Candidates who apply electronically may also have e-mail, reducing the time it takes to contact them for interviews. Applicants can be notified of the status of their applications electronically, saving time and the cost of mailing letters or postcards.

- An electronic application system will help you control the quality of your compliance recordkeeping, especially if your data includes several locations. Since all the data goes through a single system, it will be cleaner, and more valid, than if it is collected manually.

- Electronic applications will help "test" the basic computer skills of applicants for jobs which are computer-based, which these days includes most jobs.

There are also some *disadvantages* of using an electronic application process.

- If you operate in only one or two locations and have few openings and low turnover, an electronic process may be more costly than it is worth for your company. Be sure you do a cost analysis before purchasing an electronic system.

- With electronic applications, it should be "all or nothing." You will lose the efficiencies and many of the advantages of the process if you still take paper applications. Someone will still have to input the data from those applications into the system, or your applicant flow data will not be valid.

- It is critical to properly set up and install an electronic application system. Like any other computer-based system, the old "garbage in, garbage out" rule applies. Essential, or primary, job functions must be identified. Specific technical qualifications must be designated. Job codes and titles must be kept up to date. Without proper set-up and good routine maintenance, an electronic application process will not yield the expected advantages.

Screening Applications

Here are some suggestions that will help you screen applications to find the most likely candidates for your position.

- Check to make sure the application has been filled out completely and has been signed. Most people understand they must sign the employment application. If they do not sign, there is usually a reason. Experienced recruiters have found that people who do not sign the employment application will fail the drug test or have an unsatisfactory background check. It is usually a waste of time and money to proceed with someone who did not sign the application.

- Next, look at the applicant's work history. Notice the dates of employment. Look for a stable employment record with reasonable lengths of service and a continuous job and education history. Make sure all time is accounted for. If possible, have applicants list a full ten years of work and education history. If they have not worked ten years, have them start with the first time they ever worked for pay.

- Note job titles, rates of pay and reasons for leaving. As a general rule, look for applicants who would be "moving up" rather than moving backwards. When you are trying to reduce turnover, it is usually *not* a good idea to hire someone who would be taking a pay cut for doing work they have done before at a higher rate. It is also not usually a good idea to hire someone who is taking a pay cut to "change careers," especially if the career change is preceded by a period of unemployment or job hopping. Both these categories of applicants are poor risks from a turnover standpoint. Look for someone for whom your position would be better than the one they are leaving.

- Do a brief telephone interview on candidates you might be interested in, especially if it's not obvious from the application that they meet the minimum requirements for the job. When you are dealing with an out-of-town candidate, your telephone interview may take an hour or more, and will be as extensive as if that person were in your office. Again, the cost of the telephone call will be more than offset by your not having to pay travel expenses for a candidate who is not a good match for the job.

When you are talking with people by telephone about your position, try not to give them too much information about your job. You might say, "It's a clerical position similar to what you were doing at Regular Joe's." Or, you might ask, "What kind of position are you looking for?" You will be surprised how many candidates will eliminate themselves with their answer to that question. But if you give too much information too early, you will be telling the candidates in advance how they should answer your questions. The information you get will be what the applicants think you want to hear, rather than an honest expression of their needs or preferences.

One example: one time I was interviewing a young man for a safety analyst position. During the course of the interview I asked him, "If you could have any job in the world, that was absolutely perfect for you, what would that be?" He quickly and without hesitation answered "jet aircraft pilot." I knew at that point that he was telling me he was not well suited for the safety analyst position, but I ignored that intuitive feeling and hired him. He was employed for less than six months when he began trying to get a different job, and for the next 18 months total, he made my life miserable because he was so miserable.

Except for his stated preference of job, he was the 'perfect' candidate, so what went wrong? Basically, I had hired him because of his charisma, his personality; *I felt sorry for him.* He and his wife had just had a baby and he really needed a job; I could provide the job. However, his answer to the 'perfect job' question had told me that he was not at all well suited for the safety analyst position. That position required someone who was analytical and could spot problems and deal with them before people got hurt; the job he had described required someone who was willing to take risks and who craved the adrenaline rush that came with that risk. In addition, this candidate did not really like people very much. Rather than seeking people out and getting to know them, he actually blamed them for the repetitive motion injuries they had absolutely no control over.

Obviously, that was a painful lesson for me to learn, and one I've never forgotten.

If you invite candidates in for an on-site interview, tell them where to park, how long they will be there, whether they will be meeting other people and who, and if they will be taking any tests. Also, remind them to bring their photo identification and any required licenses or certifications.

During the telephone conversation, decide whether or not you want to spend any more time with them. Thank them for their time, and tell them when they will be hearing from you again. "I have several other people I need to contact before I start scheduling interviews, and that might take a couple of days." Let your notes sit for a day or two, then decide whether or not to invite them in for an interview by comparing them to your other candidates.

If you know you don't want to interview a telephone candidate, say, "I want to thank you for your time today, Suzy, but my feeling is that this job is just not going to be a good fit for you, so I don't think it'll be necessary for you to come for an interview. I appreciate your interest, though, and wish you good luck with your job search."

Testing

In many areas of the country, as many as one-third of the native-born, English-speaking applicants may not be able to read, write, or perform basic math calculations. A recent survey by the Literacy Council in one community found that fully 31% of working adults were functionally illiterate. Those numbers did _not_ include non-native-born workers and those for whom English is a second language.

Think about the implications of that. For the companies in that community, nearly one-third of their employees cannot read, write or do math at even the most basic level! And many of those employees are now in supervisory and management level jobs where they are performing poorly, much to the dismay of company executives and human resources staff.

Testing is a relatively inexpensive way to learn whether applicants really _can do_ the things they say they can do. It is an especially valuable tool when it is hard to get valid employment references. This may be the only way you have to verify specific job skills before you actually put someone on the payroll.

In many areas the state employment office, or job service, will administer basic literacy tests for you, at no charge (except what you pay in taxes, of course.) Alternatively, the adult education branch of your local school system may do basic literacy testing, also at no cost or very minimal cost.

Tests are legal when they _test skills for the job being done_, and when they _predict successful job performance_. For example, a telephone skills test would not check a press operator's skills or predict job success, but would help check skills and predict job success for a clerical job.

You can purchase tests from many different sources, but the easiest and most accurate way to make sure tests are appropriate for the job is to _create them from the job itself_. If you are testing data entry skills, give candidates samples of work, put them at a computer and have them enter the data. If you are testing drafting or design skills, give them basic information and a work space, and have them create a drawing or art piece for you.

When you do use tests as a part of your pre-employment screening, you will need to follow some basic guidelines.

- First, *test all your final candidates*, not just the ones whose skills you question. Testing some candidates and not others could open you up to charges of discrimination or unfair hiring practices.
- Wait until you have narrowed your selections down to the last two or three, and then test each of them.

- When you call them to come in for an interview, tell applicants they will be taking some tests and will need to allow plenty of time.

- Give everyone the same test. That will help you compare "apples to apples" and measure everyone by the same set of standards. It will also help prevent the perception of unfair hiring practices.

- Test in a way that is appropriate for the job. For example, give a timed test only if the actual job is timed. If you give applicants a three-minute timed data entry test when the work itself is not timed, you may be putting unnecessary stress on applicants. Instead, you might say, "It's important for you to work quickly, but accuracy is also important." Then note the start and finish times on the test while compiling the score.

- When you evaluate the tests, consider the results as a whole.

- When you score tests, set a minimum score only when you have already established that it is impossible to be successful in that job with anything less than that minimum. That would take a formal validation study lasting several months or even years. Instead, use the test scores as only one indicator of an applicant's overall qualifications for the job. Your final hiring decision will be based on a comparison of *all factors* including the candidates' work histories, education, skills, test results, reference checks and interviews.

- Be sure to keep copies of all tests you give, and keep each applicant's test results for at least one year after you fill the position. In addition, you should also keep records of actual job performance by employees in that specific job to learn whether there is any correlation between job performance and minimum test scores. This is not a difficult process, but it does require keeping records for several years.

- In addition to any tests you may give, remember to ask for copies of applicants' college or trade school transcripts. These should be sent to you directly from the school and they should be certified copies. Have candidates bring you copies of work they have done for other companies or for class projects. You will not be able to tell how much help they had from someone else, but it will be a starting place.

- You can also test by asking interview questions that will help establish specific job skills:

    "Tell me how you calculate how much raw material you will need for a 500-piece job?"

    "If you are making a sales presentation to me and I tell you I can't afford your program, how do you respond?"

> "A customer's delivery didn't get made today as scheduled and she starts screaming at you on the telephone. What do you say to her?"

All those "test" questions will help you see and hear how applicants would handle specific situations.

Even though it is a good idea to develop your own pre-employment tests, it is not necessary to reinvent the wheel. You can find lots of companies that offer standardized pre-employment tests you can use or adapt to your own needs. The Internet is a good place to begin looking.

One other test you should always give is a *drug test*, but because of the expense involved and the requirements of some federal laws, you will need to *wait* for that until *after* you have made a *conditional offer of employment*.

In summary, when you begin recruiting and screening applicants, you must first choose your recruiting method according to results you need and how much you can pay for help. Use agencies that do not require a fee for positions you can fill locally, and use executive search firms or employment agencies if you need to recruit outside your local area. When you work with an agency, make sure the agency meets your requirements for screening applicants and showing you only qualified candidates. Review the applications for employment to make sure they are completely filled out and signed, and look for stable work and education history, realistic expectations and a good job match.

Testing is a good way to establish actual job performance skills. To be legal, tests must check actual job skills and must predict job performance success. Develop your tests from the work itself and keep copies of the tests and individual results. Over a period of time, verify that there is a correlation between a minimum test score and actual job performance. And finally, include some test questions in your pre-employment interviews.

Chapter Three: Conduct a Valid Screening Interview

The next step in the hiring process is conducting pre-employment interviews.

Interviewing is one of the most commonly used selection tools, but it is also one of the *most unreliable* because there are so many variables. Some applicants are persuasive in an interview but their actual job performance is below par. Other applicants have good job performance but are not good at interviewing. In addition, some supervisors are more skilled at interviewing than others, so the quality of interviews will vary widely.

To make the most of pre-employment interviews you must take plenty of time to prepare and be disciplined about how you conduct the actual interview.

Before you begin the interview, take one last look at the candidate's application or resume and then put it away. If you use the application during the interview, you will limit the amount of new information you will get. In addition, you will get only the information the applicant wants you to have. It is much easier to get new information if the application has been taken completely out of the picture. *If you don't care about getting new information, why conduct an interview at all?*

Use a Patterned Interview

A Patterned interview has several advantages:

- Research has proven that a patterned, or structured, interview is much more effective than a random, "off-the-cuff" interview.

- It will help you conduct the same interview each time. Consistency will help you compare candidates against each other using the same criteria for each.

- The patterned interview will help you get better information from candidates in less time.

- It will help you maintain control of the interview to ensure you always get the information you need.

- It will help you avoid giving away too much information too early.

- It will help you get that crucial work history data you need in the way that you need it.

- The patterned interview will also help you maintain a legal process. It will keep you on track and help you ask only job-related questions. It will help you avoid

> Never interview from a resume or application. You'll only get the information the applicant wants you to have. Develop your own customized patterned interview and you'll get much more information.

questions that would appear to be discriminatory.

The last thing you should do to prepare for the interview is to review the list of job duties and performance standards you developed for the job, and make a list of the questions you want to ask during the interview. After you have interviewed for a single job several times, you can narrow down your list of questions. Before long, you will have a custom-designed patterned interview form that will help you get the information you need in a very short period of time.

For example, assume you're going to conduct an interview for the clerk typist position we described earlier. A few interviewing questions based on those job duties and performance standards might include:

"Give me an example of how you go about proof-reading a story. Do you have a particular method that works for you? What are some of the most common kinds of errors you see? How do you go about verifying the information in a story? What's the policy if you can't get verification? Have you ever had a conflict with a reporter because you changed something she didn't think should be changed? How did you handle that?"

Note that many of these questions, and the questions listed at the end of this chapter, are based on the applicant's prior behavior, rather than the applicant's feelings. That's because research has proved that *past behavior is the most reliable predictor of future behavior*. Rather than ask, "How do you feel about . . .?" ask, "Give me an example of a time when . . ." Rather than ask, "How do you think you would handle that situation?" ask, "Tell me about a time when . . . and explain what you did to resolve the situation."

If you need help developing a list of interview questions for your position, see the sample lists at the end of this chapter.

Now you are ready to do your interview. Take it one step at a time.

Step One:

Establish friendly control.

> Keep in mind that past behavior predicts future behavior. Therefore, base your interview questions on what has actually happened, rather than on the applicant's feelings or opinions.

This is where you take control of the interview and tell the applicant what is going to happen. Try to put the applicant at ease and establish a friendly, open communications atmosphere. For example, say, "Hello, Suzy. I'm Jane (Joe). I appreciate your coming in today. If you don't mind, I have a lot of questions I need to ask you, and I'll ask you to give me a lot of detail as we go through those questions. I'll be taking some notes as we do that. Then when we finish with my questions, I'll give you a chance to ask me any questions you might have and we'll make sure we get all those questions answered to your satisfaction. How does that sound?"

With that simple fifteen-second statement you have established that you are in control of the interview. You have told the applicant she does not need to interrupt as you go through your questions, because she will have her chance to ask questions later. Experienced interviewers who use this technique have found that it saves them between ten and thirty minutes per interview, with no loss in quality.

> If you maintain control of the interview, you should be able to decide within 20-30 minutes whether entry-level candidates are qualified.

It is helpful to note here that your purpose in conducting the interview is to learn whether the applicant is *qualified* for the open position, not to worry about whether or not the applicant likes you. During the first four parts of the interview, concentrate on getting the information you need.

Step Two:

Establish qualifications to perform the primary functions of the job, including skills, knowledge, attitude and other considerations.

Base your specific questions on the requirements of the job. For example, for the clerk typist position, you are looking for specific computer skills. Ask,

"Tell me about your experience with Microsoft Word. Which version do you use? Would you say that your proficiency is entry level, mid-level or expert? Why do you say that? Give me some examples of the kinds of work you've done using Word. Have you ever had a class or any formal training on Word? How did you back up your work? What happened if you had a problem? Did you fix it yourself or call someone else?"

Continue in this way through each of the primary functions, as well as the skills, knowledge, attitude and other requirements, until you know whether or not the applicant *can do* the primary functions of the job.

If the candidate's answers reveal that she is not qualified for your position, stop the interview here rather than continuing, unless you think she may qualify for another open position. Tell her,

"Suzy, I really appreciate the time you took to come in today, but based on your responses it just doesn't look like you meet our minimum qualifications for this job. I'll keep your application active for thirty days and call you if anything else opens up. Will that be okay?"

Let her go on with her job search while you continue looking for qualified candidates. You will save hard feelings later if you are candid with her at this point.

Step Three:

Get a **chronological work and education history.** Now that you have verified that the applicant meets the minimum skill requirements of the job, it is time to get a comprehensive work and education history. *This is a crucial section of the interview.* Done correctly, it will save you a lot of time checking references, and may keep you from hiring candidates who have not been honest with you about their work history.

If possible, get **ten years' history** on each applicant. *Ask the following questions, in this order:*

"Suzy, where were you and what were you doing ten years ago? "What was your starting date there? (Month/year) What was your job title? Briefly describe your duties. What was your pay when you started? When you left? Did you have any performance reviews while you were there? What did they say about your job performance? Did you ever have any disciplinary notices, reprimands or counseling statements while you were there? What happened? Were you ever put on probation for any reason? Who was your supervisor? What was it like working for her/him? Why did you leave? What was the last date you worked there? (Month/year) Did you give notice? Are you eligible for rehire? *What did you do next?*

All these questions are designed to get specific job performance information that will help you find the best person for the job and make your hiring decision. Use the same series of questions for each job during the past ten years.

Be sure the applicant accounts for all periods of unemployment, part-time work or school. And *be sure to start with the job ten years ago and work forward.* If there are inconsistencies or other problems with the work history, they will turn up with this method. If you start with the most recent job and work backward, you will not get the same results.

If your candidate does not have ten years of work experience, start with the last full-time school attendance. Say,

"When was the last time you were in school full time? What grade was that? Did you graduate? What classes did you take the last two years you were in school? What kind of grades did you make? When did you finish/leave school? What did you do after that? What was the first time you ever worked for pay?"

At that point, you can go to your list of work history questions and continue the process there. Remember, the more complete the information during the interview, the easier your reference checking job will be later.

Be aware, however, that if you ask questions that elicit dates, such as when an applicant last attended school full time, you could run afoul of age discrimination laws. Therefore, use the school questions only if your applicant is clearly too young to have had ten years' worth of work experience.

Before you leave this part of the interview, ask one more question: *"Have you had any other employment of any kind during the past ten years?"*

This gives the candidate one last chance to fill any gaps or correct any errors.

Total time for the interview so far should be about ten minutes for entry level positions.

Step Four:

Establish the applicant's **willingness** to do the job and **fit** for your work environment.

Now it is time to establish some rapport, and learn about the applicant's personality. What you are looking for here are the personal characteristics and cultural "fit" for your job and your company. Will the applicant be able to get along with other staff? This is especially important when you have a team environment. Will her personality style blend with or contrast with the other team members? Will she bring another layer to what you already have, or add a new dimension? Is she well suited for the type of work she will be doing?

If you have administered a personality profile before the interview, and have the results, develop a few questions designed to probe and illuminate those results.

For example, assume you are interviewing for a position that requires management of a sales staff. You know that means the ideal candidate will need to communicate effectively with people who are generally expressive, goal-oriented and focused on recognition. But your candidate's profile revealed an analytical style with a low need to nurture. You need to develop questions designed to learn whether the candidate can supervise people whose personality styles may be directly opposite hers. This is a situation that frequently creates interpersonal conflict because of the differences in style. Some questions you might ask include:

"What have you done in the past to help motivate staff members who have a high need for hand-holding and personal recognition? Give me an example of a time when you had a personality conflict with a member of your staff. What has been your approach when dealing with interpersonal conflict? Can you give me an example? Give me some examples of times when you have been operating outside your normal comfort zone."

If you have not yet administered a personality profile, you will need to learn as much as you can about the candidate's personality. The same questions will work, but you may also want to add some specifically designed to get at the basic personality style. For instance:

"Would you describe yourself as being more analytical, or more intuitive in your approach to problem solving? Can you give me some examples? Give me some examples of things that really frustrate you about people you work with. Do you see yourself as being "driven" to succeed? Why or why not? Tell me about a time when you had a conflict with a co-worker. Describe that person's personality for me. Some companies have a philosophy that includes having fun at work as a major part of their work culture. How do you feel about that? Some companies support a work environment that includes a lot of socializing with co-workers and their families. How do you feel about that?"

While certainly not as accurate as a personality profile, questions like these can tell you a lot about a person's personality, and their fit in your culture.

You are also looking for evidence of good work ethic and traits like reliability. You need to know whether candidates can be trusted to work without close supervision, or whether they will need some handholding. This is where you will ask questions designed to elicit applicants' insight about themselves, and their preferences. But you will also want to ask some specific questions designed to get at the work ethic.

Put down your note pad and pen, push your chair back and say,

"Okay, thanks. I appreciate all that information. Now we need to switch gears a bit, if you don't mind. This next group of questions is designed to help me decide whether you have the personal characteristics necessary to be successful in this job." (It helps if you can say that with a smile and an "open" or relaxed both posture.) Ask:

"How many days' work (or school) did you miss in the last two years? What's a good reason for missing work? Did you follow a particular reporting procedure when you were absent? Have you ever had any kind of warning or disciplinary notice because of absences or tardiness from work? (If yes) Tell me about that. How about when you worked at other places? Have you ever had a disciplinary notice or warning about absenteeism?"

You should always ask the "embarrassing" questions we normally think are rude or intrusive. For example,

"Have you ever been disciplined or asked to leave a job for any reason? Tell me about that, please. What do you mean by layoff? How many other people were laid off at the same time? What jobs were they in? Did you receive unemployment benefits? Have you ever had a positive result or failed a drug test? Have you ever been disciplined or warned in any way for violation of a drug or alcohol policy at work? Have you ever been disciplined or warned in any way for having a weapon at work, or for fighting or violence of any kind at work?"

"Tell me about XYZ Company. What kind of place was it? Tell me about your supervisor—what did you like/not like about him/her? If you could have the absolute perfect job for you with no restrictions, what would that job be? What would you rather do than anything else in the world?"

"Do you set goals for yourself? Tell me about some of your goals. What kind of things make you look forward to getting up in the morning? Do you prefer to be a part of a group, or would you rather be the group leader? What kinds of things frustrate you or make you angry at work? Do you have any plans to continue your education or special training?"

With attitude questions, listen for answers that tell you the candidate is *moving toward* situations, rather than moving away from them. For example, a candidate who is trying to get a job with higher pay is motivated in a positive way. A candidate who is trying to get away from a supervisor or co-worker she does not like is motivated by moving away from a bad situation, rather than moving toward growth and development. She may work hard to get a job she is not well suited for, just to get out of a bad situation. Sometimes that works out, but often it does not.

Listen for indications that candidates accept responsibility for themselves and do not blame others for their situation. Candidates who place blame and find excuses for their own situation will often be difficult to work with once hired. In general, any problems or concerns you uncover during the interview will be magnified after the employee is on the payroll.

At this point, you should have enough information to make an informed decision, and the interview should have taken no more than twenty to thirty minutes for entry-level positions.

Step Five:

Answer the applicant's questions as openly as possible.

Be sure to tell her everything she needs to know about the job in question, and give her enough information about the company to make her feel it is a good place to work. This is where you will "sell" the job opportunity and the company. Be friendly and cordial as you answer questions, and take whatever time is necessary to cover all the bases.

Step Six:

Cordial close

Remember, the applicant may be a customer, or the family member of a customer. You would like her to leave with a good feeling about the company. If possible, tell her now whether she is one of your final candidates. You might say to her,

"I've really enjoyed visiting with you today, Suzy, and at this point I'd say you're one of the top two or three candidates. I still have some other people I need to talk to, and I'll be doing your reference checks and the other things I have to do. But if I should decide that you're the person I want to hire, would you be interested in the job? When would you be available to start?"

If you know that you will not be interested in Suzy, tell her now. Say,

"Suzy, I've really enjoyed visiting with you today, but I want to be honest with you. Based on your responses to my questions, I just feel that this is not the right position for you. I sure wish you good luck in your job search, though, and if it's all right with you, I'd like to keep your application active for the next thirty days. If something else comes up during that time that I think is a better match, I'll give you a call, if that's okay?"

If you are not sure about Suzy and want to see some other people before you make a decision, tell her,

"I have several more people I need to see before I make a decision, but I will let you know one way or the other as soon as possible."

As soon as you have finished the interview, make any added notes you need to remind yourself of the candidate's strengths and weaknesses, or your concerns. Then immediately review the candidate's application, comparing the work history and other data with what you were told during the interview. Note any differences and review your notes to be sure you got everything down. Compare your interview notes to the job duties and performance standards list and make notes about the candidate's ability to meet those standards and her fit for the position. Then take a few minutes to clear your head before you start the next interview.

Professional, Management and Executive Level Positions

When you are interviewing for management, professional and executive level positions, the stakes are much higher. You have a greater investment involved in placement fees, travel expenses and relocation costs. You also have a greater potential for damage to your company if you choose the wrong person. For interviews with professional, management and executive level candidates, take the time to do a more in-depth interview than normal.

Instead of doing only a ten year employment and education history, for example, review *every* single employment and job experience, in detail, even if you are talking about thirty years or more. In addition, it is important that you *leave nothing to guesswork* and get as much information as possible about every aspect of the candidate's personality, including family influences and childhood environment. When you are considering entrusting your company's assets to a key manager, you need to know the applicant is trustworthy. The only way you will know that is by carefully probing until you are certain you know as much about that person as possible.

Open by saying,

"Rebecca, since this is such a key position in our company I need to get to know you as well as possible in this situation. I'm going to ask you dozens of very detailed, personal questions that are designed to help me to do that. I'd appreciate it if you'd be as candid as possible with me so we can both be sure this job is a good fit for you. We may take several hours to do all this, and we'll take a break if we need to. When we get finished with all my questions, I'll give you the opportunity to ask me all the questions you have about the job, the company, and the people you'll be working with. We'll take whatever time we need to do that, and I'll be as candid with you as I've asked you to be with me. Are you ready to get started?

Begin the management and executive level interviews with questions about childhood experiences and the family environment.

"Where did you grow up? What kind of work did your parents do? Did you have brothers and sisters? What were your parents like? What sorts of things did you do as a child? As a teenager? What was it like growing up in your family? At what point did you decide to become an (engineer, accountant, etc.)? Did you always know with certainty what you were going to do with your life? Who/what influenced you to do what you are doing? Why did you change your mind about being an engineer/accountant, etc.?"

Next, move on to school experiences and ask equally detailed questions about every aspect of school and college.

"What kind of classes did you take in school? Any favorites? Tell me about your favorite teacher. How about the teacher you hated the most? Which classes were the easiest for you? Hardest? What kind of grades did you make? Did you participate in any extra-curricular activities? What did you learn about yourself through those experiences? How did you pay for college? Why did you choose XYZ School? Did you work while you were going to college? Did you have any honors or awards while you were in college?"

Follow that with a detailed work history, probing in great detail every aspect of every job.

Remember to ask the key questions to establish the continuity of work/education time:

"Why did you decide to leave there? What was the last day you worked? (Month and year) Did you give notice? How much? Are you eligible for rehire? *What did you do next?*"

If candidates say they can't remember the specifics, give them some time to think about it, but do not allow them to look at their notes or write anything down. It will be *critically important* for you to compare the verbal responses with the written resume or Application for Employment once the interview is complete. *If there are issues with the dates of employment, jobs not mentioned, or fabricated work history, this is where you will uncover them.*

"What made you take the first job with XYX Company? What did you think it would be like there? And how was it? What was your first job assignment? Who did you report to? What was his/her title? Describe your duties and responsibilities for me. What did you accomplish in that job that you felt good about? Any mistakes you'd like a chance to do over again? What was your next assignment? How did that come about?"

Continue probing for this level of detail into every aspect of an executive candidate's personal and work history until you feel you know that person as well as it is possible to know someone without living or working with them for years. You need to know how candidates respond to adversity, how they handle themselves in crisis situations, how they see themselves in relation to the rest of the world, and whether or not they are basically optimistic and forward thinking.

You need to learn whether candidates believe they are self-determining, or believe they do not have much control over what happens to them. Research has proven that people who believe they are self-determining will accept accountability for their own actions and not try to blame others or "circumstances" when things go wrong. They will also be more likely to push for results even when some risk is involved.

You need to know if applicants have personal preferences, or prejudices, concerning people, moral and ethical situations, and the role of business or education in our society. Are their beliefs compatible with yours? Can they bring something new to the team in a positive, constructive way, or will the differences create conflict and unnecessary turmoil? All these questions must be answered. Of course, they won't be answered at all unless you have created a Patterned Interview process in advance of the interview.

Often, it is not possible to answer all these questions in a single interview. For professional, management and executive level positions it may be necessary to have candidates come back for a second, third or even fourth interview. For executive positions, it is important to get spouses involved in the process, particularly if the spouses fill a supplemental entertainment role or help with the company activities.

And for all professional, management and executive level positions, it is a good idea to involve other people in the company in the interviewing process. One way to do that is to have several key people spend thirty or forty-five minutes each with candidates who have passed initial muster and have been invited back for the second or third interview. When you do this, set up a schedule in advance, tell candidates who they will be seeing and what their positions are, then have each interviewer fill out an evaluation form on each candidate. Exposing candidates to several different personalities is a good way to determine team fit. If there are any obvious problems, it is better to find them during the interview process rather than after someone has been hired.

If the candidate has traveled from out of town, you will need to allow time on the first trip for all these things to happen. That may mean two or three consecutive days of on-site time for the applicant. And it will mean that a comprehensive schedule for the entire duration of the trip will need to be developed. If necessary, contact a realtor whom you trust to give a comprehensive tour of the city and overview of the real estate situation.

When other people are to be involved in the interviewing process, make sure they have all been trained in interviewing and have some basic interviewing skills. Give each of them a copy of the Job Duties and Performance Standards. Make sure they have been well versed on legal issues involved in hiring so they don't ask questions that are out of line and could land you in court.

Finally, try to have the interviewing process reflect the working environment. For example, if people in your company work in teams, interview your candidates in teams for at least part of the process. If the position you are trying to fill is on the evening or night shift, do at least one interview during those hours, in that environment. If the position requires heavy travel, do part of the interviewing away from home and observe how the person adapts to travel situations.

About the number of on-site interviews: All "on-site" interviews do not have to be conducted "on-site." Some may be over lunch or coffee at a convenient local restaurant. Some may be at a group gathering or team meeting at a hotel or conference center. Some may be over breakfast or at an airport meeting place. The more variety you can bring to the situation, the less stressful it will be for candidates who must meet several people and go through several interviews for a position. Take into consideration the location, whether a candidate is likely to be recognized, and the level of position. You do not want to jeopardize a candidate's current position by being too public, but there are times when privacy is a sure giveaway that there is an interview going on.

Interviewing Guidelines

Here are some general guidelines about pre-employment interviewing, without regard to the level of the position:

- First and foremost, remember that your primary focus must be on determining *whether or not the candidate is a good match for your job.* Avoid falling into the trap of trying to please everyone. Yes, we are all taught to be nice to others, and we want to do that. But we do not have to carry that so far as to try and find a reason for hiring every candidate. Rather, look for areas where the candidate does *not* match your job profile, and save "nice" for the last two steps in the interview process. Until then, it is your job to control the interview, follow your patterned process, and get the information you need to make a decision.

- Avoid telling candidates too much about the position before you begin your interview. When you give people a lot of detail about the job, you tell them, in effect, how they need to answer your questions. Say, "It's a sales position similar to what you're doing now. I'll give you more detail when we get together." If candidates ask about pay before they agree to come for an interview, respond by saying, "It's hard to set a specific rate until I know more about your qualifications. Did you have a particular rate in mind?" Of course, if you do have a single, specific rate such as for all entry level jobs, go ahead and tell candidates what that rate is.

- Limit your questions to those that are job related. List your questions in advance (patterned interview form) and work from that list. By doing that, you will not be tempted to stray off into areas that could cause legal problems. See Resources for more information on questions you should avoid asking.

- Use closed questions when you need a "yes" or "no" answer. "Can you pass a drug test?" When did you work at XYZ Company?" Use open or indirect questions when you need reasons, feelings or explanations. "Tell me how you felt about that. Why did you decide to leave?"

- Talk less than twenty percent of the time. If you're doing the talking, you're not learning anything.

- Be sure you make no promises. Comments like, "Oh, nobody ever gets fired here," could create a contract situation you don't have the authority to fulfill, especially if you maintain at-will employment at your company.

- Find a private place for the interview. Close the door and ask someone to hold your telephone calls. Turn off your cell phone and electronic gadgets. Interruptions will cost you time and loss of concentration, and will be irritating for the applicant.

- Establish a climate that will encourage applicants to be open and candid with you. One way you can do that is by establishing an informal setting for the interview. If you interview from behind your desk, with candidates sitting across the desk from you, the desk creates a formality and distance that makes it difficult to establish a communications connection. Move to a conference table and interview across the corner of the table, or from the same side of the table. If you can reasonably get your chair to within three feet of the candidates, it is easier to establish and maintain eye contact and a soft, natural, conversational tone of voice. If candidates are having a hard time relaxing, invite them to remove their jackets and walk with you to get a cup of coffee. Take them on a tour of the facility. If none of these suggestions work, try moving to a completely neutral place, like a local restaurant.

- Be open about your note taking. Candidates need to know that what they tell you will be checked. Say, "I'm interviewing several people for this position and want to be sure to remember the important things about each person. That means I'll be taking a lot of notes, so just ignore that, okay?"

- If candidates cannot remember details of their work history, say, "Well, take a few minutes to think about it, if you'd like. This is really important, and we can't go on until we get this done." If the candidate says, "Didn't I put that on my application?" respond, "Yes, I'm sure you did, but if you don't mind I'd like you to tell me again." In any event, make sure the applicant gives you a complete work and education history *during the interview* so you can later compare it with the written application. Again, this is one of the most critical parts of the entire interview.

- Structure your questions so the applicant cannot guess at the answer you are looking for. For example, if you ask, "Are you willing to work third shift?" applicants will almost always say "Yes," especially if you have advertised for a third shift job. But if you ask, "Do you have a shift preference?" applicants may say, "Well, I'd really like to work first shift." If you ask, "What shift do you prefer?" applicants might tell you, "I'd really rather work first," on the off chance you might have a first shift job open. Even better: "Does it make any difference to you what hours you work?" or "What hours would you like to work?" These questions will tell you whether your applicant really is willing to work third shift, or whether the applicant is only telling you what you want to hear.

- *Past behavior is the best predictor of future behavior.* That is why experts recommend that you ask for examples of actual behavior. For instance, rather than say, "How do you think you would respond in that situation?" say, "Give me an example of a time when . . ." or "Describe what happened when you . . ." There are more "behavior based" questions in the lists on the following pages.

- Use silence. It is not necessary to fill every moment with words. Instead of making a comment or asking another question immediately, just smile and nod your head a bit. That will encourage the applicant to keep talking. This is an especially effective tool when you have asked an open question that requires some thought on the part of the applicants. They will often give you a glib answer first, and then your silence will encourage them to be more honest, or to express a second thought.

- When trying to determine whether the candidate's personality is a good fit for the job, remember that personality traits generally do not change substantially over the years. Behaviors, however, can be changed. One issue you need to take into consideration is the extent to which candidates will be operating *outside their normal comfort zone*—or personality traits—and how difficult or stressful it would be for them to modify their behaviors. According to the research, many people are able to operate outside their primary style for a period of time if their motivation is strong enough. But just how far outside is too far? *A close match is necessary for long-term effectiveness.*

- Be sure to notify all applicants when the job has been filled. People who have had an interview should receive either a telephone call or a signed letter. People who responded to an advertisement should receive a postcard or form letter.

- Never tell applicants that they "weren't qualified," or someone else was "better qualified." They will want to know why, and you may eventually have to prove your statement in court. A better approach is to say, "I was impressed with your background, but I felt this position was just not right for you. I'd like to keep your application . . ." If the candidate was a finalist but you selected someone else, you might say, "It was a very difficult decision because I had several very well-qualified applicants, but I did want to let you know I've offered the job to someone else. Could I keep your application active in case something else comes up?" Try not to make comparisons between applicants, but limit your comments to the candidate's own situation. If the candidate is insistent, say, "It wasn't any one or two things, but a combination of everything. Based on my experience and your responses to my questions, I think this is just not the right position for you."

- Remember, you are your company. The way you treat applicants during the screening and hiring process, and especially during the interviewing process, will determine how they feel about and how they talk about your company in your community. Maintain high standards of professionalism at all times, and treat people as you would want to be treated in the same circumstances.

Developing Interviewing Questions

Different kinds of interviewing questions have specific uses during an interview. It's important to use the right kind of question for each part of the interview.

Use closed, direct questions when you need specific, right-to-the-point answers. For example:

"Can you pass a drug test?"

"Have you ever been convicted of a felony?"

"Did you complete your college degree and graduate?"

"When did you leave that company?"

"How often did you exceed your performance goals?"

Use open, indirect questions when you need opinions and attitudes, or when you need complete descriptions. For example:

"Tell me about your experience with working on second shift."

"Describe what happened that caused you to be fired."

"Explain the procedures you follow when you shut down at the end of the day."

"Give me your impressions about your last supervisor."

"How do you feel about working closely with a group, versus working on your own?"

Ask probing, follow-up questions when the candidate has said something of interest but did not elaborate. For example:

"That's interesting, tell me more about that."

"Why do you say that?"

"Oh?"

"Explain that for me, please."

"Tell me what you mean by 'standing over you'."

When you are interviewing, you are trying to learn whether the applicant really *can do* the job, really *will do* the job, and is a *good fit* for the working environment you have to offer.

Here are some sample questions to help you find the answers to those questions. Use these samples as a starting place to develop your own questions, based on the specifics of your particular job. The questions are not listed in any special order.

Behavior-based can do questions: (soliciting specific examples of past behaviors)

"Tell me about the work you do/did for XYZ Company."

"What was a typical day like for you?"

"How did you learn to do that?"

"What kind of training did you have?"

"How much of your time was spent doing that?"

"Which of the things you did were the most difficult? Easiest? Most fun?"

"What did you like most/least about that job?"

"How did your supervisor evaluate your performance?"

"Describe that process for me, please."

"Which elements of the job do you think you do/did best?"

"Where do/did you need to improve?"

"What kind of decisions do/did you make during the course of your work?"

"Did you have specific performance standards? How did your work compare to those standards?"

"How was the quality of your work measured?"

"Were there written procedures or policies for your job?"

"Whom did you go to when something came up that was outside the normal operating procedures?"

"Did you do your work by yourself, or were there other people involved?"

"Describe your chain of command for me."

"Tell me about some of the things you accomplished in that job."

"Did you ever suggest any changes in the work that would result in a better way of doing things? What were your results?"

"Describe the step-by-step procedures you used to start up each day."

"Has there ever been a time when . . . describe that for me, please."

"Give me an example of a time when you had a conflict with one of your supervisors or a co-worker. Tell me about that, please."

"Have you ever walked off a job and quit without notice?"

"Tell me about a time when you set a goal for yourself and then achieved it."

"How about a time when you set a goal and then *didn't* achieve it?"

"Describe your time management system for me, please."

"Tell me about your follow-up practices with customers."

Will do and fit questions: (soliciting attitude and feelings)

"If you could have any job in the world, with no restrictions whatsoever, what would that job be?"

"If you had the freedom to design the perfect job for yourself, what would it include?"

"How would you describe your supervisor?"

"What kind of things do you do in your off-work time?"

"Tell me about things you've done that make you feel the greatest sense of accomplishment."

"Other than the work itself, what things do you look for in a job or a place to work?"

"How many times were you absent from work during the past two years, and for what reasons?"

"Do you have a preference about the hours you work?"

"Physically, what the most difficult thing you've ever done?"

"Have you ever quit or walked off a job without giving notice? Tell me what happened."

"Describe the perfect supervisor."

"Have you ever had a situation where your supervisor asked you to do something you didn't think you should do? Tell me about that situation. How did you handle it?"

"Have you ever worked an evening or night shift job? Rotating shift or hours? Variable schedule?"

"If you have your choice between working in a job where you control most aspects of your work yourself, or in a job where you have to depend on several other people for part of the work, which would you prefer and why?"

"What descriptive words or phrases do you use to describe yourself?"

"What kinds of goals have you set for yourself?"

"When you look back at yourself when you were in school, are you surprised by where you are and what you're doing now?"

"What kinds of things make you angry? Happy?"

"Who has had the greatest influence on you? Why?"

"Would you rather work by yourself or in a team of other people? Why?"

"If there were something you could do over again, what would that be?"

"As far as your career progress in comparison to the rest of your school classmates, how are you doing?"

"Can you point to a particular time or event in your life that became a turning point for you?"

"Have you ever shopped in my store? (On the Web site?) Tell me about your experience."

"Do you have any preferences about the type of people you work with?"

"Have you ever been fired or asked to leave a job or company for any reason?"

"When compared to your current job, what would it take for you to find a better job?"

"What kind of income do you want to have in five years?"

"What motivates you?"

"Why do you think you would do well here?"

"If hired here, how will you transfer skills from your last job?"

"What would your top priorities be during your first week? In a month? In a year?"

"Why should we hire you?"

"If we hire you, how long do you see yourself staying in this position?"

Of course, the author is not suggesting that you use all these questions for every candidate; your interviews would be hours long! Instead, choose a few questions from each different section to include in your Patterned Interview Form, then use the same questions for every interview. Consistency is important, and the Patterned Interview process will help you be consistent.

In addition to these questions, you should study the section on avoiding legal problems during the hiring process in Chapter Four. That chapter gives you specific information about questions that have been found to be discriminatory and resulted in payment of damages to applicants. By knowing in advance what to avoid, you can prevent such problems in your company.

Chapter Four: Employment Law in Hiring

As a business owner or manager, one of your most important jobs is creating an environment where people can do good work. In fact, that's a good definition of "leadership." You make it possible for your company to meet or exceed your operating goals when you create a productive, professional workplace, where people respect and value each other.

There is another reason you must be concerned about the working environment, and that is the law. There are dozens of Federal and State laws that govern how we treat applicants for employment. Failure to obey these laws can cost the company hundreds of thousands—even millions—of dollars in fines and lost revenues. It can result in disastrous relationships with your employees, customers and vendors. And in some cases, it can result in monetary fines *you would personally* be forced to pay.

The purpose of this chapter is to tell you briefly what you need to know about these laws so you can protect yourself and your company's assets. These laws are very complex, so there is no way you can get all the information you need in this short chapter. Also, keep in mind the author is not an attorney, so you should only use this section as a reference. When questions come up, ask your company's legal counsel for advice.

First, *it is illegal* to make decisions about applicants or employees on the basis of race, religion, color, age, gender, national origin, handicap, disability or veteran status. Any decisions about hiring must be made *without consideration* of any of these factors or you could be charged with discrimination.

Further, you must make sure there is *no sexual harassment or discrimination* in the hiring process. Take a brief look at some of the major laws that affect the hiring process.

Age Discrimination in Employment Act

Protects employees and applicants who are between the ages of 40 and 75.

Americans with Disabilities Act

Requires access and reasonable accommodation for disabled or handicapped people who are *otherwise qualified* to perform the essential functions of a job. Forbids discrimination because of handicap or disability. *Prohibits pre-offer questions* about health or physical disability.

Civil Rights Act of 1964

This law makes it illegal to base employment decisions on race, color, national origin, religion, sex (gender) or pregnancy. Penalties include both compensatory and punitive damages. This law also specifically prohibits sexual harassment, which is defined as *"creating a hostile or intimidating work environment."*

Department of Transportation Drug Testing Requirements

Requires certain employers to conduct drug tests of some employees and to provide education and assistance for recovery from drug addiction.

Drug-Free Workplace Act

Establishes guidelines for a drug-free awareness program and requires that certain companies make a good faith effort to carry out the program. *Requires penalties or rehabilitation* for employees convicted of workplace drug offenses.

Employee Polygraph Protection Act

Generally prohibits the use of polygraph tests in an employment situation. There are some limited exceptions.

Employment at Will

Most state laws still allow companies to operate on an at-will basis, meaning there is no guarantee of length of employment or terms or conditions of employment. Both the company and the employees may decide to terminate employment at any time, with or without notice, and with or without a reason. Companies that maintain at-will employment can still offer limited employment contracts.

Equal Pay Act

Prohibits pay differentials on the basis of gender for substantially equal work that requires equal skill, effort and responsibility under similar working conditions.

Fair Credit Reporting Act

Requires that companies notify applicants and employees of intent to use investigative consumer reports, and disclose the scope of the investigation. Also includes some credit reporting requirements.

Fair Labor Standards Act

Sets the minimum wage. For hourly-paid employees, requires payment of overtime at the rate of time and one-half the regular hourly rate for all hours worked in excess of forty in a week. Requires accurate records of time worked for hourly employees. Also includes some restrictions on use of child labor. State laws on the payment of overtime may vary, so check the laws in your state.

Family and Medical Leave Act

Covers companies with more than fifteen employees. Eligible employees must be given up to twelve weeks of unpaid leave in a twelve month period in case of serious illness of the employee or the employee's spouse, child or parent. It also includes birth or adoption of a child. Eligibility applies to a *male or female* who has been employed twelve months and has worked 1,250 hours in that twelve month period. Requires a guaranteed return to work in a position of equal pay and status, with no loss of benefits. It is illegal to discriminate against an applicant who has taken advantage of the FMLA benefits.

Federal Military Selective Service Act

Gives employees returning from US Military service the same wages, benefits and rights they would have received had they not left. Also bars discrimination against members of the Reserves and the National Guard.

Immigration Reform and Control Act

Prohibits hiring of illegal aliens. Requires verification and record keeping of identity and work authorization documents.

Privacy Act of 1974

This Federal law and many State laws prohibit release of employee medical information except under strict guidelines. Along with HIPPA, limits some inquiries during the pre-employment process.

Penalties for non-compliance of these employment laws vary according to the specific law, but may include actual monetary damages in the form of back wages, "front wages," fines, and even double fines when the violation is found to be deliberate. The complaining party's attorney fees, the company's attorney fees and court costs must be paid. Punitive damages may be assessed, especially by a jury if a case goes to a civil trial. The company may be forced to hire, reinstate, promote or increase the pay for wronged employees or applicants. Customers and advertisers may refuse to do business with the company because of negative publicity. In the case of sexual harassment, individual supervisors and managers may be held *personally liable* for monetary damages.

Aside from the financial costs of failure to comply with employment laws, there are employee morale issues. Employees want to feel they're being treated fairly by a company's supervisors and managers. When there is a perception of unfair treatment, morale and productivity suffer, company loyalty drops, attitudes turn bad and turnover increases. Conflicts escalate between employees, and customer service declines. Trust becomes a scare commodity, and people start looking for problems instead of paying attention to business.

How to prevent problems in hiring

Here are some things you can do during the hiring process to prevent problems and to make sure your company is in full compliance with the applicable laws.

- During the pre-employment process, always recruit and advertise in the "general help wanted," "clerical," "professional" or "management" categories. Avoid using terms in your ads like young, energetic, male, female, white, Caucasian, boy, girl, married or single. Always include the phrase "Equal Opportunity Employer. Make your job titles generic—press operator instead of pressman.

- Always use more than one recruiting method to avoid claims that you unnecessarily restrict applicants. If you only use employee referrals, and your work force is primarily white, for example, you may be excluding qualified minorities from applying.

- Treat all applicants alike. If you use tests, test all final candidates, not just the ones about whom you have a question. Use the same interview for everyone. Base your interviews on a patterned interview for consistency. Check references on all final candidates, not just those about whom you have concerns.

- Avoid asking interview questions that may be perceived by applicants as discriminatory. Ask only job-related questions. If you use a team interviewing process, be sure other members of the team understand which questions they should avoid.

- Maintain contacts with minority and female organizations that might help you recruit. Develop good relationships with these groups so they will send you qualified applicants.

- Never ask applicants to submit photographs. Ask for documents that show an applicant's age *only after* a job offer has been made, unless there is a bona fide requirement. For example, if a job requires a valid driver's license and current insurance coverage, you may ask for those documents during the pre-employment process.

- Never comment on an applicant's appearance or physical characteristics, even if it is obvious there is a handicap or disability of some kind. Explain to all applicants the physical requirements of a job and ask if they can meet those requirements. Leave it up to applicants to tell you if they will need a reasonable accommodation and what that accommodation might be. Your job is to determine whether applicants are qualified to perform the primary duties and responsibilities of the job. Concentrate on that and let the rest take care of itself.

- Protect the privacy of applicants. Results of drug tests, references and background checks must never be released. Put paperwork and files in a secure, private place. Leave it up to applicants to tell people why they were not hired. Say, "I'm sorry, that's a private matter between your son and the company. You'll have to ask him about that."

- When checking references, limit your questions to things that are specifically job related. Don't make comments or ask questions about personal characteristics or physical features. Be careful about how you describe the job and the company, and don't make promises you may not be able to keep.

- Notify applicants on a timely basis of the status of their applications. If you have done a good job with your recruiting and interviewing, a lot of unsuccessful applicants will be eager to hear their results. It is rude and inconsiderate to keep them wondering too long.

- Treat applicants the way you would want to be treated, or the way you want a member of your family to be treated. Even candidates who do not have a ghost of a chance of being hired should be treated with dignity and respect. A smile and genuine courtesy will go a long way to diffuse potential problems.

Interviewing danger zones

During the pre-employment interview, it is especially important that you avoid asking questions or making comments that could be perceived as biased or discriminatory. None of the questions listed below are discriminatory by themselves, but since they are not job-related they could leave applicants with a negative impression. In addition, some of these questions would raise a doubt about how you intend to use the information if not for a discriminatory purpose.

Don't Ask:	Ask Instead:
How old are you? What is your age? What is your date of birth?	Are you at least 18 years of age?
When did you graduate from high school/college?	Did you graduate? If we should make an offer of employment, can you have the school send us a certified transcript?
What is your marital status? Are you married? Are you divorced?	There are no acceptable questions. This is not a job issue!
What is your maiden name?	We need to verify your work history. Have you ever worked under any other name?
What does your husband do for a living?	There is no acceptable question about a spouse.
How many children do you have? How old are they? Boys or girls?	If you're concerned about attendance, ask, "How many days' work did you miss in the last two years?" Otherwise, do not ask questions about children.
Do you and your spouse plan to start a family?	Don't ask. This is not job related.
Who takes care of your children while you're working?	This job requires attendance every day from 8 a.m. to 5 p.m., with occasional evening overtime. Will you be able to work those hours?
Where were you born? Where were your parents born? What language do you speak at home?	This is not a job related issue. Don't ask. Can you speak, understand and read English?
Are you a U.S. citizen?	Can you prove that you're legally able to work in this country?

Review these questions with other employees who might talk with applicants who come in to interview. Teach these employees *not* to ask the questions that are not job related, even in "casual conversation." These casual conversations are as much a part of the interview as your formal question and answer session. Several companies have been found guilty of discrimination at least in part because of questions that were asked by non-supervisory staff during casual conversation.

On the other hand, sometimes applicants themselves will mention "the unmentionables," such as spouse, children or church activities. If applicants do voluntarily bring up these subjects, you may talk about them. Not to do so would be rude and insensitive, and would seriously hinder your ability to establish a reasonable rapport with the applicant. Just be sure you never base any of your hiring decisions on these factors, and take care with any notes you make. Remember, everything is "discoverable" in court.

But be sure the interviewers include the conversation in their notes, along with a mention of how the conversation got started. Memories fade and often interviewers simply cannot remember a specific conversation unless they have made careful and comprehensive notes.

> A commercial background-checking firm's study revealed that 11.5% of employment applicants had a criminal record. The categories:
>
> 35% auto offenses
>
> 21% theft/fraud
>
> 15% alcohol and narcotics
>
> 15% threatened violence

> *A major service provider performed 2.1 million background checks and found that 44% of applicants had lied about their work histories. 41% lied about their education and 23% falsified credentials or licenses.*

Chapter Five: Check References and Make the Job Offer

It is unfortunate, but in today's competitive market, many applicants resort to half-truths, omissions and even outright lies to make their application and resume more appealing to potential employers. A study by a major executive recruiting firm revealed that as many as *seventy percent of the professional and management-level resumes* they received had been *falsified* in some way. The figure was closer to *thirty-five percent* for entry-level positions. In a recent survey of college seniors who were about to graduate, *forty-eight percent* of participants admitted that they "had lied on their resume or application to get a job."

The most common kinds of alteration are:

- Changing dates of employment. Applicants will change dates to make it appear their job history is more stable than it is, to cover up a period of unemployment, or to hide a short-term job they don't want you to know about.

- Altering education. Candidates will claim a college degree they never completed, a school they never attended or a course of study they never took. Rather than admit they left school after only three semesters, they may claim a bachelor's degree. They may claim a 3.0 or better grade point average when it was much less. In some cases, applicants have been found to have never been enrolled at a school where they claim to have completed a degree. At entry levels, it is common for applicants to claim they graduated from high school or completed a General Education Diploma (GED) equivalency program when they did not. Some liberal arts graduates have claimed a science degree to qualify for a particular job.

- Adding or omitting employers. It is common for job applicants to not list companies from where they were fired, or where they worked only a few weeks or months. Less common but still frequent is listing as a former employer a company where the candidate never worked. Again, the attempt is to improve the work history and help the applicant get an interview.

- Changing job titles, duties and rates of pay. Many applicants think they can "promote" themselves by listing their current or former job title and pay rate as substantially higher than they really are. Bookkeepers become office managers; maintenance helpers become journeyman electricians. Data entry operators become programmer analysts. Pay rates get changed from $8 per hour to $18 per hour, or from $560 biweekly to $560 weekly. Annual salaries may be inflated by 20 to 30 percent. The common thought pattern is that most companies want to give new employees a step up to come to work for them and pay and job titles are often based on the current or last previous pay and job title. Applicants think they can get farther ahead by bumping up their job title and pay history.

- Change reasons for leaving. Many applicants who were fired from a previous job for poor performance or excessive absenteeism will change that reason for leaving on their application to "layoff" or "better job." Sometimes they will admit they were fired but will lie about the reasons for the termination.

> A psychology professor at the University of California Medical School found that "most people cannot tell from demeanor whether someone is lying or telling the truth—but most people think they can."

- Lying about a criminal record. Contrary to popular belief, it is not discriminatory to refuse to hire a convicted felon for a job related reason. For example, for a cash handling position you would not want to hire someone who had been convicted of theft, fraud or embezzlement. For a position that requires driving a company vehicle you would not want to hire someone who had been convicted of felony driving under the influence. Make sure the "Have you ever been convicted of a felony?" question on the application has been answered and then ask the question again during the interview.

Exercise Due Diligence

What is the big deal if someone wants to alter their resume or job application? Two things. First, you and your employees need to know the people you will be working with are who they say they are. You need to be able to trust them, to count on them to keep their word. You need to feel safe both at the work place and at home. You need to develop good interpersonal relationships and teamwork with your employees and co-workers. None of these things is

> In the United States, there are six million threats of violence and two million workplace assaults each year. Thirteen people die every week due to workplace violence. Workplace violence has become the number one cause of employee death at work.

possible with people who will lie on their resume or job application.

Second, in many states companies are being held accountable for making sure the people they dire are who they claim to be. It is called "due diligence," and it means you have done everything you possibly can do to verify references and background information. Companies that have been found negligent in their hiring practices have paid a heavy price in workplace violence, stiff fines and astronomical civil court judgments.

Too protect yourself and your co-workers, and to protect the assets of the company, you must make sure you have checked references before you put a new employee on the payroll. The following guidelines will help you with that process.

- Be sure to distinguish between references, and court records or background checks. The two are completely separate. The reference check is something you will do to verify the education, skills and work history of your applicants. It involves calling previous employers, requesting official transcripts and otherwise verifying the information on the application and given during the interview. A court records check includes a criminal records check and credit report and should be done on any final candidate for a cash handling or supervisory position, a position that involves working with youth, disabled or elderly individuals, and in some cases positions that involve public or customer contact. In most areas, this can be done by calling the county court house and asking for a review of the official records in any counties where the applicant has lived. If you are not able to do it, you can pay someone else to do it for you. The court records check does not substitute for the reference check; both must be done.

- Don't waste your time with "personal" references. The references you need are always those that are job related, and preferably provided by a former or current supervisor. You may use military discharge papers to substitute for one of those references, but be sure you also talk to at least one or two former supervisors, either inside or outside the military.

- Never substitute letters of reference or other written documents for reference checking. Documents are easily forged. Letterhead can be "borrowed" and signatures can be easily copied, especially with current technology. Any documents you accept should be certified with a raised seal and mailed directly to you from the issuing institution.
- Start by making sure the Application for Employment has been completely filled out and signed. As noted earlier, there should be no exceptions here.

- During the pre-employment interview, carefully follow the interviewing procedures suggested, particularly in the section dealing with the work and education history. Any inconsistencies or hesitancy on the part of applicants may mean there is reason for concern; you will want to check those areas especially carefully.

- Get the names and telephone numbers of current and former supervisors. You can promise not to call those people for references "without your permission," but hesitancy to give you those names may mean there is a problem.

> Experts say it's especially important to do complete background and reference checks for management and executive position candidates. The applicants are often so intelligent and engaging that their candor and credibility seem beyond reproach. They are more likely to get away with lying than more entry-level candidates.

- Always ask a few "problem" questions during the interview. "Have you ever been fired or asked to leave a job or company? Have you ever had any kind of disciplinary action or warning notice at work? Have you ever been suspended or sent home from work?" "Is there anything else I need to know about you before I start checking your references?" Always remind final candidates that you will be checking their references.

- After you finish an interview always take a few minutes to review your notes and compare them to the information on the resume or job application. Any differences at all should raise a red flag. Some discrepancies are more severe than others, but all should be checked. For example, if a hire or termination date is off by a month, or even a year, it may be a mistake, especially if the error carries through the entire work history. On the other hand, a difference of several months or a year in several places in the work history would be a major problem. Use your judgment here, but check everything.

- Make a list of questions you need to have answered during the reference checking process. Use the same basic list of questions for all your applicants, with only a few minor changes for the individuals involved. Your list will keep you from leaving out important data and will help you compare one candidate to another.

- Ask for specific verification of things the applicant told you during the interview. "He said . . . can you verify that?"

Frequently, companies will be reluctant to release reference information, or will release only the job title and dates of employment. If that happens, say, "I have a signed authorization and *release from liability from him.* May I fax that to you?" Sometimes the release from liability will get you the information you need.

Or, since most states now have laws releasing companies from liability when they provide references, you might say,

"I'm calling for an employment reference in accordance with Arkansas Act 1474 (or your state's law). As you know, that Act releases your company from liability when you provide references in accordance with the Act. John Doe has given me written authorization and a release from liability to get a reference from your company. Are you authorized to release this information?"

> Approximately 38 states have now enacted laws providing liability protection for companies giving pre-employment reference, when the information given is "truthful, factual, and given in good faith." Check your state's law.

Another method that sometimes gets what you need is asking if you can send them a form to fill out. When you fax a list of your reference questions, be sure to fax a copy of the job application with the release from liability highlighted.

You can sometimes get more actual job performance data from a supervisor than from someone in the human resources office. When you make your call, ask for the supervisor by name rather than saying you need to check an employment reference. When you reach the supervisor, say,

"Joe has given me permission to talk to you about a confidential employment reference. Is this a good time for you to answer a few questions?" If it is not a good time, ask, "May I call you at home?" If the supervisor says, "We're not supposed to give references. You need to talk to the human resources office," try, "Okay, I can do that, but I thought it would be all right since Joe did give me permission to talk to you."

When you do find someone who will talk to you, ask specific, job related questions. Phrase your questions objectively so they don't indicate what your concerns might be. And *do everything you can to make sure the information is truthful, verified, and used in good faith.* For example,

"How many days' work did he miss last year?" is much better than "Did he have an attendance problem?" Even better: "What do your records show about his attendance during the last year?"

"If you evaluated his job performance, what kind of quality rating did he receive?" Better: "What do your records show about the results of his performance evaluations?"

"According to the file, did he maintain a positive attitude toward you, the company and his co-workers?"

"Did you ever have to take any disciplinary action or give him any reprimands or performance reminders of any kind?"

"Why did he leave?"

"Is he eligible for rehire?"

"Do you know what he did next?"

Those are all good, objective questions that are obviously job related.

It's always a good idea to ask the reference to pull their personnel file, if possible. Begin your questions with, "Can you give me his dates of employment, please?" "What does the file say about how many days' work he missed last year?" (You won't want to start a management, professional or executive level job with this question.)

Continue with other questions by asking specifically what is in the official record.

Another good technique is to verify data the applicant gave you. For example, "Joe said that he was certified on the CNC machine, and has been operating that for about a year. Can you verify that?" Follow that question up with things like, "Did he meet his quality objectives? What was his re-work rate? Was he able to work without close supervision?"

Finally, to complete your due diligence, always ask about drugs and violence. For example, "Did Joe ever have any disciplinary notices or other problems with drugs or violence against employees? Was he in compliance with the company's drug and alcohol policy? Were there ever any incidents involving weapons, violence or threats of violence against other employees or supervisors?"

Before you finish a reference call, there are two more questions you should always ask. First: "What did he do after he left your company?" This question will often yield completely new information the applicant has not given you. Unfortunately, that is usually not good news.

Second: "Is there anything else you'd like me to know about Joe before I make my decision?" That question gives references a chance to comment in an area you may not have asked about. For example, you might hear something like, "Well, I guess he told you he got fired from here. But I really think what happened had more to do with his family situation than anything else. If he's got that worked out, he could probably be a good employee again."

This is information you might not have known about, since you couldn't ask about Joe's family situation during the interview. Unless he volunteered the information, you would have no way to know this might have been a factor in his losing the earlier job. If several years have passed and his situation has stabilized, you might want to take that into consideration.

Another example of something you might hear is, "He told everybody around here that he had another job when he left. But I know the guy he was supposed to go to work for, and as far as I know, that never happened. I don't know if the job fell through or what, but I think he's been out of work for quite a while." The applicant may have listed "another job" as his reason for leaving and also listed the new employer as if he actually went to work there.

Sometimes, no matter what you do, you just cannot seem to get the reference information you need. Let caution be your guide here. You should *never* hire a candidate on whom you were not able to get at least two positive, completely satisfactory references. Three is better.

There may be a situation where you have to go back to a candidate and say, "Joe, I'm just not going to be able to make you a job offer unless I can get the references I need. Is there anything you can do to help us out here?"

Sometimes a phone call or personal visit from the applicant will convince the references to release the information. And there may be a situation where you must *refuse to hire* someone because you could not get the reference information you need. It is much better to do that than it is to hire someone and regret it later.

If it is necessary to refuse to hire because of bad references or no references, it is a good idea to protect your sources when you can. For example, say,

"Joe, I'm not going to be able to hire you. After a lot of consideration I've come to the conclusion that this job is just not the right match for you." If the candidate asks for details, say,

"A lot of things go into that decision, but what it boils down to is my judgment that this is just not the right situation for you."

You can follow that up with a general statement about keeping the application active in case something else comes along, but avoid giving a candidate hope of a future job if there is no hope at all.

If you tell candidates they were not hired because of bad references, though, you will have a terrible time ever getting another reference from that company.

Be sure to protect the privacy of job applicants to avoid running afoul of Privacy Act requirements. Treat every application with confidentiality through every step of the process. If you decide not to hire someone because of poor references, a bad credit history or failed drug test, you must never reveal that information to anyone. You will take some heat, especially if the applicant was an employee referral or family member. But that is better than embarrassing someone and causing problems for yourself and your company because you revealed something you should have kept confidential.

In case you still think all this reference checking is overkill, let's look at a couple of examples where a little reference checking would have prevented real problems.

Arkansas Act 1474 became law largely because of a single incident in which a disgruntled employee took guns to work and killed and wounded several co-workers, including a supervisor. The investigation revealed that the worker's former employer, Company B, had terminated his employment because he had brought a gun to work in violation of company policy. However, when the current employer, Company A, had called for a reference, Company B did not release the reason for the termination. A judge later found *Company B guilty of negligence for not exercising due diligence* and informing potential employers of the reason for termination. The court, and later an appeals court, both affirmed that the Company B had a duty to protect the public. The fines assessed were significant, and were followed by a Civil court judgment against Company B for negligence.

In another case, in a major city, a Director of Training who at the time was president of the local chapter of the American Society for Training and Development, (ASTD) announced at a Chapter meeting that he would be leaving his current employer, a large oil company, to begin a private training and development consulting business. He was subsequently contacted by a local manufacturing company to do a comprehensive Needs Analysis. The "consultant," whose business cards and resume` introduced him as having earned a Ph.D. in Industrial Psychology, was to develop a proposal that would be presented to the Board of Directors for approval. When the consultant was unable to complete the proposal, reference checks revealed that he had been terminated from his previous position as Director of Training for "having falsified his application for employment."

In fact, the consultant did not complete a Ph.D. at all—he had been in prison (for fraud) during the years when he claimed to be in school, and the highest grade he had actually completed was when he received his high school equivalency certificate, or GED, several years after he should have graduated high school. He had never attended college at all, except for the correspondence courses he had completed while in prison. In addition, he was functionally illiterate.

In this case, the two professional employees who had hired him for the Needs Analysis both suffered severe career setbacks that damaged their reputations and caused significant embarrassment and loss of confidence. It all could have been avoided if they had checked the consultant's references before hiring him to do the project.

Making an Offer of Employment

All offers of employment should be made "contingent upon our getting satisfactory results on the references, drug test and background check." Ideally you will have completed at least the references before making the offer, especially on candidates who will need to give notice to their current employer. Then, make arrangements for the drug test and background check as soon as possible. If candidates live in another city, have these things done while they are in town for the interview or house-hunting trip.

You should never allow someone to begin work until these things have been completed. If you do let someone start to work before all the references, drug test results and background check have been received you may find yourself in the unpleasant situation of having to terminate the employment of a brand new worker. In addition to the cost of making a mistake like this, it can be embarrassing for everyone involved and has been known to result in fraudulent hiring lawsuits, especially if the candidate left another job to come to work for you.

Also, be careful how you refer to the job. If you maintain at-will employment, you might hire someone for a *full-time, part-time or temporary position*, but *not* for a *permanent position*. Employees might be paid by the hour, or paid a bi-weekly salary, but *never* paid an *annual salary*. You might refer to a benefits *waiting period* of 90 days, or an *orientation* period, but if you maintain at-will employment there is *no probationary period*.

When you make a job offer by telephone, take a few minutes before you call to review your notes and make a list of the items you need to cover. At a minimum, you will want to include starting date, starting pay, job title and hours of work. You may also want to emphasize any benefits like time off with pay and medical insurance, and say what the eligibility requirements are. If you are willing to pay a hiring bonus or relocation expenses, mention those.

To save a little time, use a new hire checklist as a guide. It will help you cover everything you need to cover.

For professional, management and executive level positions always follow up a verbal offer with a written offer. Astute applicants will be reluctant to give notice to their current employers until they have your written offer in hand. Again, be aware of the legal implications of the language you use, and don't make promises you are not prepared to keep.

If you do decide to give someone an employment contract, make sure all the terms are spelled out in detail and the contract has been approved in advance by your legal counsel.

Finally, in both your verbal and written offers, remember to tell prospective employees how much you are looking forward to working with them and "sell" the company. Make sure their questions have been answered and they know how to get in touch with you if other questions come up before they start to work.

And sell, sell, sell. It is common for applicants to have second thoughts after they have accepted your offer, and even after they have given notice to their current employers. Be sure you have made that transition as easy for them as possible.

Chapter Six
What's Next?

Now that you have good people on the payroll, it is important that you provide the kind of working environment that will keep them on the job and prevent future turnover. This will become even more important in the future, when forecasters are predicting an eight million person shortage of labor. When you are competing in a labor market as tight as it is forecast to be, you cannot afford to make a mistake.

Here are some suggestions you can use to make sure your working environment is as employee-friendly as possible, without costing your company a fortune.

New Hire Training

- Pay especially close attention to new employees during their first few days, weeks and months after hire. You have already invested a lot of time, energy and money in these new people, and very likely one of the reasons your offer was accepted was that you made the candidates feel important, and wanted. Make sure that good, positive feeling continues once they are on the payroll.

- Develop a self-directed orientation plan for new hires to use as they become acquainted with the company. Self-directed plans are important because different people learn and accomplish at different rates. One-size-fits-all does not work. An example of an Orientation Checklist is included in the following section.

- Assign new employees a buddy, or mentor, to help steer them through the first few days and weeks. This person will help the "newbie" learn about the company culture and make sure they are included in the informal gatherings that take place. New employees will ask a buddy questions they won't ask a supervisor or manager. Turnover will be lower because new employees will more quickly feel they "belong."

- When selecting buddies or mentors, be sure the employees you choose have an unfailingly positive attitude, and genuinely enjoy helping other people. You want someone who shares your philosophies regarding work ethic issues, is on top of morale issues, and is well respected throughout the company.

- Implement a formal New Employee Orientation training program. This is a great opportunity to get new employees started by hearing your story, in the way you want it told. Orientation programs will vary according to your company's needs, but you'll find an outline that was used by one manufacturing company in the Resources section.

- In all of your new hire training efforts, make sure you explain to employees, up front, what will be expected of them each step of the way. Establish high standards, with specific outcomes. Use evaluations as a way to review and double-check progress.

The Work Environment

- In research study after study, employees have said they want a work environment where they can be challenged, where they can make a real contribution, where their contributions are recognized and rewarded, and where they can learn new skills. Take a look at the environment in your company. Ask yourself if you can answer "yes" to each of those factors. If not, immediately begin to change those things that need to be changed.

- Invest in leadership development programs for your supervisors and managers. These first- and middle-level managers are the ones who determine the *real* work environment, as opposed to the one you hope you have. Supervision today, and into the foreseeable future, is a far different proposition than it was only five or ten years ago. If you are not giving these key staff members the update training they need, you are doing both them and yourself a great disservice.

- Conduct an annual or semi-annual employee opinion survey, and then make the changes needed to maintain your competitive edge. Employees will tell you things in an anonymous survey that they will not tell you in person. The results will have more validity than the opinions of a few outspoken people. But be prepared to implement necessary changes, or employees will resent the fact that you asked and then refused to take action. There are many good sources for inexpensive, benchmarked opinion surveys. It does not have to be rocket science to be valuable.

- Review your pay, benefits, performance management, rewards and recognition programs to make sure they are accomplishing what you really want them to accomplish. All these programs—called "total rewards" programs—are key to retaining the employees you need. But they need to be designed so that they reward the right kind of performance. For example, there is certainly nothing wrong with recognizing longevity with a service pin. But if your goal is to increase productivity, then you need to be recognizing superior performance rather than years of service. Ask your senior human resources professional or a qualified consultant to guide you in this area. Chances are you are too close to be objective.

- Conduct exit interviews with every terminating employee, whether the termination was voluntary or involuntary. These exit interviews must be done by someone other than the immediate supervisor and her immediate manager. If you do not have a human resources staff, consider outsourcing this function to a qualified consultant or outsourcing provider. Compile and report the exit interview information at least quarterly. One company implemented exit interviews and found that while most voluntary terminations cited "more money" as their primary reason for leaving, the next three things listed were "lack of training," "poor job training" and "poor supervision." Appropriate programs were implemented and new hire turnover immediately began dropping.
- Consider implementing a team environment, if that is appropriate for your company. Studies have shown that when properly applied, employee creativity, problem solving and productivity will increase in a team environment, while voluntary turnover will decrease. It goes back to the employees' need for challenge, feedback and continuous learning. And there is a strong element of not wanting to let team members down by leaving the company. Even if a full-fledged team environment is not appropriate for your company, look for ways to use short-term project groups that can be assigned a specific task and held accountable for its satisfactory completion. And remember that team rewards have different requirements than individual rewards.
- Remember that it is impossible to communicate *too* much with employees, especially if you want them to care about your business. Except for proprietary or regulated financial data, the more you share with employees about the business

and their role in its success, the more they will be able to contribute to the bottom line. Spend time with employees in *their* work space, getting to know them and talking about the business. Share operating goals and results with them. Talk constantly about every aspect of the business. They will feel more involved and connected, and will contribute at a higher level than if they feel cut off from information.

- Create ways to give employees instant or near-instant feedback about their individual and group performance. One company saw an immediate 15% reduction in scrap when they began having operators calculate their own productivity throughout each day. Remember, employees pay attention to what you pay attention to. And when they calculate their own results, they see the impact they are having on the business.

- Be flexible. This will become more and more important during the next few years as the market adjusts to a real labor shortage. You will need to re-think issues like how work is scheduled, what an "ideal" candidate looks like, how work can be done, *where* work can be done, and by whom. Look for older workers asking for part-time or seasonal work as they ease into a more active retirement than in past years. How can you accommodate those potential employees in your work place? To the extent you can do that, you will be well ahead of the competition in the search for talent.

- Invest in skills development and personal growth training for employees. Even as the average length of employment has dropped to less than two years, employees will be more likely to stay with a company where they can continue to develop their technical and personal skills. They will be more productive, and effective, while they are with you. Your company will reap the benefits of employees who are continuously learning and growing.

Obviously, these suggestions are easier to think about than to do. Some are more difficult than others. But there are plenty of low cost ways to provide a productive, motivating work environment. Make the commitment for your company, or for your department, and you will see an immediate payback.

As you have discovered now that you have worked your way through Part One, Hiring Right is more than just placing an ad in the newspaper and doing a quick interview on the resulting flood of applicants. It requires careful, advance preparation. It requires a methodical, patterned approach to interviewing. And it requires that you diligently check everything you have been told by applicants.

But the payoff for spending the time required to follow the recommended process can be huge, both for yourself and for your company. When you hire correctly and make a good match of the candidate to the job, your turnover costs will go down, and your productivity and profits will go up.

Best of all, as a hiring manager or human resources professional, you will have peace of mind knowing that you have done a complete, thorough job and given yourself and your company a legitimate chance for success.

Now continue on to **Part Two**, where you'll find complete *blueprints* for hiring office clerical workers, entry level labor, technical staff, sales staff, and workforce managers. These blueprints include forms, patterned interviews, orientation plans, and more.

For questions, feedback and additional resources check out our Web site at www.patkelleyauthor.net

Part Two

Business Blueprints

Blueprint One
A Business Blueprint™ for Hiring Office Clerical Workers

1. **Complete a Job Profile,** or use the following Office Clerical Job Profile.

2. **Develop a newspaper ad** (see below) and/or a flyer to circulate to current employees and local schools and colleges.

Just Starting Out?

Join a company where the skills you bring are more important than years of experience!

Full time, entry level administrative position in a busy insurance office. Perform data entry, handle mail and correspondence, prepare routine reports. *Requires proficiency in Microsoft Office 2010 or later.* Starting pay $9.00 per hour. Benefits after three months. Pre-hire test and drug test required.

If you're a self-starter who loves a challenge and knows how to set priorities, we want to talk to you! Apply on-line at www.yourcompany.com

Equal Opportunity Employer

3. Email job opening notices to the State employment office and the local Community College or Vo-Tech placement office.

4. Post the job internally and/or on the company's Web site. Include qualifying questions to eliminate applicants who are not qualified.

5. Screen applications.

6. Conduct telephone interviews. See Chapter Two, Recruiting and Screening Applicants.

7. Schedule interviews for internal applicants and employee referrals. Ask applicants to allow time for testing, or ask applicants to complete on-line tests before the scheduled interview time.

8. Administer on-site testing, or review results of on-line tests. For this position, use data entry, Microsoft Office suite, proofreading and math. Create tests from probable work or purchase standardized tests. If possible, include a validated personality profile.

9. Conduct on-site interviews. See the attached Patterned Interview.

10. For the top two or three candidates, schedule second interviews with Hiring Manager.

11. Complete telephone or mail reference checks on the final candidate or candidates.

12. Complete the credit and background reports on the final candidate.

13. Make a conditional job offer, contingent upon completion of final pre-hire activities.

14. Send the final candidate for a drug test, review results.

15. Call the final candidate with a confirmed job offer. Send the confirmation letter.

16. Receive acceptance of offer and schedule New Employee Orientation.

17. Notify unsuccessful applicants that the job has been filled. Remove job postings from all sites.

18. Develop a New Employee Checklist for the position.

Forms Needed

- Completed job Profile
- Patterned Interview
- Telephone Reference Check
- Written Reference check
- New Employee Orientation Checklist
- Other new hire forms as required

Office Clerical Job Profile

Primary Duties

Perform computer data entry on items such as accounts payable and receivable, payroll hours work, new hire paperwork and employee status changes, plus other items as assigned. 40%

Answer multi-line telephone, route calls, respond to help requests, take and relay messages. Follow up to be sure help requests have been given prompt response. 15%

Type, proofread and prepare documents for mail or shipping. Sort and distribute daily mail. Prepare outgoing mail and items for shipping. 15%

Gather data from multiple sources and prepare routine monthly management reports for approval. 20%

Verify billings for equipment and supplies. Order, receive and distribute department supplies. 5%

Provide administrative support for up to six professional employees. provide customer service for user departments as needed. Maintain files for all work. 5%

Secondary Duties

Provide back-up support for payroll clerk as needed. Up to 10%

Other duties as assigned or required.

Performance Standards

Data entry is 100% error free. All work is proofed and checked before being transmitted or finalized. All normal deadlines are met.

Provides excellent customer service both internally and externally. Telephone is answered before the third ring. No complaints.

All work is error-free when it leaves the department.

All routine deadlines are met.

Supplies are always in stock on an as-needed basis. Billing errors and caught prior to payment.

Monthly reports are accurate and error-free. Problems are brought to the manager's attention immediately. No surprises. All deadlines are met.

All files are current and correct.

All users evaluate support as "meets requirements" or better. No complaints are received.

Must be able to speak, read and write English with clarity and perform basic math at the 10th grade level.

Payroll work is timely and error-free.

Knowledge, Skills and Attitudes

Completion of Microsoft Office 97 or above training. Demonstrated proficiency in Word, Excel and PowerPoint is required. Above average grammar, spelling and proofreading skills are required.

Proven outstanding customer service skills are required. Proven ability to work without close supervision, meet multiple deadlines, and prioritize work under competing demands is required. Professional appearance and demeanor are required.

Six months' work experience in an office clerical environment, with a variety of duties and customer service responsibilities, is preferred.

Work Environment

Position is situated in a busy office where a variety of work is done. Office includes seven other staff. Teamwork is required to accomplish tasks on a timely basis. Work area is open and noisy with a variety of conversations and operating equipment. Priorities often change quickly, with very little notice. High levels of quality and productivity are required.

Physical Requirements

Must be able physically to operate a computer keyboard, telephone and variety of office equipment, including fax and copy machines. Must be able to hear, see, and speak with clarity. Lifting is less than five pounds and infrequent.

Personal Qualities

Must enjoy a fast pace. Must be challenged by quality and productivity demands without becoming overly stressed.

Must be able to work alone for extended periods, without close supervision. Must be able to concentrate on data, identify and isolate problems. Must be able to provide error-free work without undue frustration or impatience.

Must also be able to work as a member of a team when required.

97% attendance and 100% punctuality are required because of the volume of the work.

Must enjoy providing exceptional customer service, both to internal and external customers.

Must be flexible. A sense of humor is highly desirable.

Completed by: (name and job title)   date

Approved by: (name and job title)   date

Clerical Patterned Interview

Introduction: "Hello, (applicant's name) thanks for coming in. I appreciate your interest in (Company name). If you don't mind, I have a lot of questions for you, and I need you to answer them in a lot of detail. I'll be taking some notes so I can remember what we talk about, so don't worry about that, and you're welcome to take notes as well. We may take about twenty minutes or so for my part. When I'm finished, I'll give you a chance to ask me any questions you have, and we'll take whatever time we need to make sure everything is answered to your satisfaction. How does that sound?"

Qualifications Questions

Tell me about your training and work experience with the Microsoft Office suite of products. Which version do you use?

Give me some examples of the types of work you did using those products.

Would you say that your proficiency is entry level, mid-level or expert level? Why?

How did you back up your work?

What did you do if you had a problem?

Have you ever operated a multi-line telephone? What kind of system was it?

Have you ever had any experience with proof-reading, either your own work or someone else's?

Describe your experience, if any, with handling several projects at the same time, when they're all due at once. How did you decide what to do? How did it work out?

Have you ever had a situation where you were trying to please several people at the same time? Tell me about that.

Hiring Right   Pat Kelley

What happened?

What kind of grades did you make in school? In English? In math? What was the highest level class you took in
English? In math?

Have you ever had any office procedures classes? How did you do?

Did you ever have a class where you thought you received a lower grade than you earned? Tell me about that, please.

Has there ever been a time when you were being held to a higher standard than you thought was possible or realistic?
Tell me about that?

What have you discovered about your work abilities and limitations?

How do you define "stress"?

Please tell me about any experience you've had in a customer service position.

Did you ever have a time when a customer yelled at you or complained about the way you did something? Tell me about that. How did you feel about the way it turned out?

Education and Work Experience
(Assumes little or no experience for this
entry level position)

Please tell me about all your formal education, beginning with high school.
Did you graduate?

What was the first time you ever got paid for doing a job? When did you start? (month and year)

When did you leave? (month/year)

What was your job title? Your duties?

What was your pay when you started?

What was your pay when you left?

Did you have any performance reviews while you were there?

What did they say about your job performance?

Did you ever have any disciplinary notices, reprimands or counseling statements while you were there? What happened?

Were you ever put on probation for any reason?

Who was your supervisor? (Name, phone number)

What was it like working for him/her?

Why did you leave?

Did you give notice?

Are you eligible for rehire?

What did you do next?

When did you start? (month and year)

When did you leave? (month/year)

What was your job title? Your duties?

What was your pay when you started?

What was your pay when you left?

Did you have any performance reviews while you were there?

What did they say about your job performance?

Did you ever have any disciplinary notices, reprimands or counseling statements while you were there? What happened?

Were you ever put on probation for any reason?

Who was your supervisor? (Name, phone number)

What was it like working for him/her?

Why did you leave?

Did you give notice?

Are you eligible for rehire?

What did you do next?

Repeat the same sequence of questions for each period of work, unemployment or school, accounting for high school or the last time school was attended, through the last job, or at least ten years. If needed, add separate additional pages.

Have you had any other employment of any kind during the past ten years that we haven't talked about? If yes, repeat the sequence of questions.

Decision Point: *Is the candidate technically qualified?* If so, continue with the interview as shown below. If not, terminate the interview now. Say "(Applicant's name), I really appreciate your coming in today but, based on your answers, you do not meet the minimum qualifications for this position. Would you like me to keep your application on file in case something else comes up in the next few weeks?" Escort the applicant out, give a cordial good-bye. If the applicant is technically qualified, continue with the interview:

Willingness and Fit

How many days' work did you miss in the last two years?

What's a good reason for missing work?

Did you follow a particular reporting procedure when you were absent?

Have you ever had any kind of warning or disciplinary notice because of absences or tardiness from work?

Have you ever had a positive result, or failed a drug test that was work related?

Have you ever been disciplined or warned in any way for violation of a drug or alcohol policy at work?

Tell me about (Company name where candidate works or worked). What kind of place is/was it?

Tell me about your supervisor. What did you like or not like about him/her?

If you could have the absolute perfect job for you, with no restrictions, what would that job be? Why?

Do you set goals for yourself? Tell me about some of your goals. Did you achieve them? Why or why not?
What kinds of things make you look forward to getting up in the mornings?

Do you prefer to work as part of a group, where your work depends on other people in the group, or would you rather work in a situation where the only person you have to depend on is yourself?

What kinds of things frustrate or make you angry at work?

Have you ever had a situation where you were part of a group, and you got your work done but the rest of the group didn't. Were you penalized because of them? What happened?

I'm going to give you some words. Please tell me if they describe you or not, and why.
    Analytical?
    Ambitious?
    Laid Back?
    Amiable?
    Considerate?
    Fun-loving?
    Fearless?

Given a choice between staying home with a good book and going out to a party with friends, which would you choose? Why?

What kinds of things do you do for fun?

One last question. What else can you tell me about yourself before I make my decision?

Answer the Applicant's Questions. Note the Questions below:

Cordial Close—Explain the next steps in the process and the timeline to complete these steps.

Interview Results

Is the candidate qualified?   Yes No   If no, why not?

Referred to Hiring Manager for Interview?   Yes No   Date Referred?

Personality Profile Completed Date   _____
Acceptable?   Yes   No

Skills Test Completed Date   _____
Acceptable?   Yes   No

References Completed Date   _____
Acceptable?   Yes   No

Credit Check Completed Date   _____
Acceptable?   Yes   No

Background Check Completed Date   _____
Acceptable?   Yes   No

Drug Test Results Date   _____
Acceptable?   Yes   No

Conditional Offer of Employment Date Made _____
Details
- Telephone
- Mail
- Job Title
- Reports to
- Starting Pay
- Location

Offer Accepted Date _____ Start Date _____ Date
Confirmed Start _____

Attach Forms:
- Job Duties and Performance Standards with Signatures
- Application for Employment, Signed
- Patterned Interview form, Date Completed
- Tests and Test Results
- Drug Test Results
- New Employee Orientation checklist, Date Completed
- IRS Form W-2
- Request for Job Modification, Date Completed, Actions Taken

    Of course it is impossible for me to include every single contingency you will want on your interviewing and new hire documents. If you are like most managers, you will probably modify and revise your forms and process several times before you are completely satisfied. Because of that, it is always a good idea to keep, or have an assistant keep, a project file that details all the steps you went through and all the changes you made over time. That way, if you are ever audited by the EEOC or another Federal or State regulator, it will be easy for you to show them your files. Just remember that memories fade over time. Do not rely on your memory being better than the average manager's.

New Employee Orientation Checklist

Week One:

1. Complete the new hire paperwork, including the Employee Handbook and Code of Conduct. Initial and date when complete.

2. Receive benefits materials and review benefits. Initial and date when complete.

3. Complete the New Employee Orientation Program. Attach copy of Certificate of Completion.

4. Receive tour of facility, meet co-workers, receive keys, learn timekeeping system. Begin clocking in and out for shifts.

5. Review Orientation Checklist, understand responsibility for properly completing Checklist. Review Job description and Performance Standards. Initial and date when complete.

6. Receive operating system authorization. Set up in system and secure password entered. Initial and date when completed.

7. Learn where supplies are kept. Review purchasing procedures. Correctly complete a basic office supply requisition and purchase authorization. Initial and date when complete.

8. Begin tutorial on data operating system. Complete Module One. Initial and date when complete with 100% accuracy.

9. Learn where procedures and manuals are kept. Study department and Company policies and procedures. Study required forms and complete them correctly. Initial and date when complete.

10. Receive instruction on telephone system. Correctly receive and route an incoming call. Initial and date when complete.

11. Continue tutorial on operating system. Modules 1-8 complete with acceptable scores by the end of Week One. Initial and Date when complete.

Week Two:

12. Review first week with supervisor, ask/answer questions. Initial and date when complete.

13. Continue with study and completion of operating system modules. Complete Modules 9-14 with acceptable results. Attach copy of Certificate of Completion.

14. Meet individually with add department staff to discuss their specific responsibilities. Initial and date when complete.

15. Schedule and participate in meetings with key interface staff in other departments to discuss their responsibilities and needs. Complete all meetings during the week. Initial and date when complete.

Week Three:

16. Review first two weeks with supervisor, ask questions. Initial and date when complete .

17. Assume normal job duties and responsibilities.

18. Meet with supervisor at the end of the week to assess progress and answer questions, and to resolve any issues. Initial and date when complete.

19. Issue Certificate of Completion for New Employee Orientation. Copy of certificate and Checklist signed and filed in employee's personnel file.

Hiring Right *Pat Kelley*

Blueprint Two
A Business Blueprint™ for Hiring Entry Level Labor

1. Complete a Job Profile, or use the following Entry Level Labor Job Profile.

2. Develop a newspaper ad (see below) and/or a flyer to circulate to current employees and local agencies.

Job Hunting?

Move UP to a factory where your opinion counts, and where pay increases are based on your job performance rather than seniority. Start on second or third shift, work without direct supervision after training. Move up based on your work record and willingness to keep learning. Great place, great people.

Must be able to read and speak English and do basic math. Drug free workplace. Pre-employment testing required.

Apply in person ONLY at the Job Service office, 900 Garrison Avenue, Fort Smith.

Equal Opportunity Employer

---

3. Email job opening notices to the State Job Service and local placement offices. Review hiring procedures with employment office staff. Provide them with a supply of applications and required skill tests. Establish a window for taking applications.

4. Screen applications and schedule on-site interviews.

5. Conduct on-site interviews. (See the attached patterned interview.) Schedule second interviews with Hiring Manager.

6. Complete telephone or mail reference checks on the final candidates.

7. Complete background reports on final applicants.

8. Make a conditional job offer (conditional upon completion of final pre-hire activities. Send final candidate for a drug test.

9. Call final applicant with a confirmed job offer. Schedule New Employment Orientation.

10. Notify unsuccessful applicants that the job has been filled. Remove job postings from all sites.

11. Develop a New Employee checklist for the position.

Forms Needed:

- Completed Job Profile and Performance Standards
- Patterned Interview
- Telephone Reference Check
- Written Reference Check
- New Employee Orientation Checklist
- Other new hire forms as required

Entry Level Labor Job Profile

Primary Duties

Perform a variety of non-skilled duties relating to production and/or assembly of manufactured parts.

Track and calculate productivity, waste and quality.

Perform routine housekeeping tasks to keep work area neat and clean.

Comply with all safety guidelines.

Participate in team meetings for problem solving and productivity.

Knowledge, Skills and Aptitudes

Requires six months' previous factory experience. Must be able to speak, read and write English with clarity and perform basic math at the 8th grade level. Previous experience working evening or night shift preferred.

Work Environment

Factory is somewhat noisy. Safety hazards include moving equipment such as forklifts, automated equipment and moving production line.

Physical Requirements

Must be physically able to bend, reach, stoop, handle parts, see and hear 100% of the time. Must be able to move and lift up to 30 pounds frequently throughout the shift.

Personal Qualities

Must be able to tolerate a continuously fast pace.

Must be challenged by quality and productivity demands without becoming overly stressed.

Must be able to work alone for extended periods, without close supervision.

Must be able to comply with all policies, procedures and standards including attendance, punctuality, productivity, safety, waste and quality.

Must be able to work as a member of a team when required.

(Insert signatures and dates)

Entry Level Labor Patterned Interview

Introduction

Hello (name), thanks for coming in. I appreciate your interest in (Company Name). If you don't mind, I have a lot of questions for you, and I need you to answer them in a lot of detail. I'll be taking some notes, so don't worry about that. We may take about 20 minutes or so for my part. When I get finished, I'll give you a chance to ask me any questions you have, and we'll take whatever time we need to make sure everything is answered to your satisfaction. How does that sound? Okay, let's get started.

Qualification Questions:

Tell me about your factory experience.

What was a normal day like for you?

Did you meet your quality and productivity standards?

How did you get help if you had a problem?

What kind of grades did you make in school? In English? In math? What was the highest level class you took in English? In math?

How do you calculate a percentage? What's 32% of 175?

Has there ever been a time when you were held to a higher standard than you thought was possible or realistic? Tell me about that, please.

What have you discovered about your work abilities and limitations?

Do you have a shift preference?

Have you ever worked a shift other than days? Tell me about that experience please.

What's the most difficult physical work you've ever done?

Tell me about your experiences working with a group or team of people where the team as a whole was required to produce a certain result.

Have you ever had a conflict with someone at work? What happened? How did it work out?

Why are you applying for a factory job?

Why do you want to work at this company?

Education and Work Experience (assumes little or no experience for this entry-level position)

Please tell me all about all your formal education, beginning with grade school. Did you graduate from high school? When and where?

What was the first time you ever got paid for doing a job? (Alternate question for experience workers: Where were you and what were you doing ten years ago?)

When did you start? Month and year?

When did you leave? Month and year?

What was your job title?

What were your duties?

What was your pay when you started?

What was your pay when you left?

Did you have any performance reviews while you were there?
What did they say about your job performance?

Did you ever have any disciplinary notices, reprimands or counseling statements while you were there? What happened?

Were you ever put on probation for any reason?

Why did you leave?
Did you give notice?

Are you eligible for rehire?

What did you do next?

Repeat this sequence of questions for each period of work, unemployment or school. Account for high school or last time school was attended, through the last job, or at least 10 years.

Have you had any other employment of any kind during the past 10 years that we haven't talked about? (If yes, repeat the sequence of questions.)

Decision Point: Is the candidate technically qualified? If so, continue with the interview. If not, terminate the interview now. Say, "(Applicant's name), I really appreciate your coming in today, but based on your answers you do not meet the minimum qualifications for this position. Would you like me to keep your application on file in case something comes up in the next few weeks?"

Notes:

Willingness and Fit

How many days' work did you miss in the last two years?

What's a good reason for missing work?

Did you follow a particular reporting procedure when you were absent?

Have you ever had any kind of warning or disciplinary notice because of absences or tardiness from work?

Have you ever been fired or asked to leave a job for any reason?

Have you ever had a positive result, or failed a drug test that was work related?

Have you ever been disciplined or warned in any way for having a weapon at work, or for fighting or violence of any kind at work?

Tell me about (company name). What kind of place was it?

Tell me about your supervisor. What did you like or not like about him or her?

If you could have the absolute perfect job for you, with no restrictions at all, what would that job be? Why?

Do you set goals for yourself? Tell me about some of your goals. Did you achieve them? Why or why not?

What kinds of things make you look forward to getting up in the mornings?

Do you prefer to work as part of a group, where your work depends on other people in the group, or would you rather work in a situation where the only person you have to depend on is yourself?

What kinds of things frustrate or make you angry at work?

Have you ever had a situation where you were part of a group, and you got your work done but the rest of the group didn't? Were you penalized because of them? What happened?

I'm going to give you some words. Please tell me if they describe you or not, and why.
Analytical?   Ambitious?   Laid back?

Amiable?   Considerate?   Fun-loving?

Fearless?

Given a choice between staying home with a good book or going out to a party with friends, which would you choose? Why?

What kinds of things do you do for fun?

One last question. What else can you tell me about yourself before I make my decision?

Say, "Okay, (name), I really appreciate your patience in answering all these questions for me. Now, what questions do you have for me?

Answer the Applicant's Questions. Note the questions.

Cordial Close: Explain the next steps in the process. Let the applicant know when she should expect to hear from you. Thank her for her time.

Entry Level Labor
New Employee Orientation Checklist

Day One:

1. Complete new hire paperwork including Employee Handbook and any required forms.

2. Receive benefits materials and review benefits.

3. Complete New Employee Orientation Program.

4. Receive ID badge, meet co-workers, learn the timekeeping system. Begin clocking in and out.

5. Receive and sign for personal protective equipment. Learn how to use PPE.

6. Review the Orientation Checklist, understand responsibility for properly completing the Checklist. Review job description and performance standards.

Day Two:

7. Meet with supervisor, assign training mentor, begin training.

8. Schedule for any required training.

9. Assume normal duties and responsibilities under supervision of trainer or mentor.

10. Meet with supervisor for any questions or concerns.

Day Three:

11. Assume normal job duties.

Hiring Right   Pat Kelley

Blueprint Three
A Business Blueprint™
for Hiring Technicians

1. Complete a Job Profile, or use the one illustrated.

2. Develop a newspaper ad and/or a flyer to circulate to current employees, and to the local schools and colleges. Place in technical or general help wanted, Sunday only. Set as Display, two columns by 3". Review and approve a draft in advance of run date.

Quality Assurance Technician

No room to advance? We're an employee-friendly company offering exceptional career growth for the right candidate.

Full-time position reports to QA Manager. Responsible for Six Sigma program administration. Requires two years' experience in a Six Sigma certified environment. Bachelor's degree and Black Belt preferred.

Pre-employment and drug test required. Must provide current references and certified transcripts of all college work and special training.

Apply on-line at www.yourcompany.com

Equal Opportunity Employer

---

5. Screen applications. Eliminate those which do not qualify. (See Chapter Two, Recruiting and Screening Applicants.)

6. Administer on-site testing, or review results of on-line tests. For this position, include math and knowledge of Six Sigma fundamentals. Create tests from probable work or purchase standardized tests. If possible, include a validated personality profile.

7. Conduct telephone interviews. (Chapter Two).

8. Schedule on-site interviews. Ask applicants to allow time for testing, or require applicants to complete on-line tests before the scheduled on-site interview. Interview only those who meet the minimum criteria.

9. Conduct on-site interviews using a patterned interview. See sample below.

10. Complete telephone or mail reference checks on final three candidates. Schedule second interviews with the Hiring Manager.

11. Coordinate Hiring Manager interviews.

12. Complete credit and background reports on the final applicant.

13. Make a conditional job offer. If accepted, schedule applicant for drug test. Send a confirmation letter to the successful applicant.
14. Receive acceptance and schedule start date and new Employee Orientation.

15. Notify unsuccessful applicants that the job has been filled. Remove job postings from all sites.

16. Develop a New Employee Orientation Checklist for the position.

Forms Needed

- Completed Job Profile
- Patterned Interview
- Telephone Reference Check
- Written Reference Check
- New Employee Orientation Checklist
- Other new hire forms as required

Technical Job Profile

Primary Duties:

Administers Six Sigma quality program. Includes training employees, monitoring production results, conducting lab and factory floor testing, and producing required documentation and reporting.

Works closely with QA Manager and other staff to produce and implement quality program guidelines and standards.

Develops and conducts DFSS training for employees to teach teams the Six Sigma concepts and application.

Applies Six Sigma processes to daily production work.

Develops and implements policies and procedures to advance Six Sigma principles throughout the plant.

Recommends preventive measures to prevent problems.

Works closely with production and engineering staff to troubleshoot problems as they arise.

Secondary Duties

May participate in management meetings in the absence of the QA Manager.

Other duties as assigned.

Performance Standards

Company adheres to all requirements for continued Six Sigma certification.
Demonstrates continuous improvement in achieving quality goals.

Is respected by all employees. Demonstrates good interpersonal skills.

Training results achieve stated outcomes.

Work is pro-active and forward-looking.

Documentation is clear and easy to follow. Writing meets acceptable standards for clarity and accuracy.

Demonstrated skill in applying control chart, defect measurement, Pareto, process mapping and root cause analysis to solve problems.

Complies with all policies and procedures.

Knowledge, Skills and Aptitudes

Must be able to demonstrate expert-level knowledge and skill in all aspects of Six Sigma quality programs. *Required*.

Speak, read and write English with clarity, and accurately perform advanced mathematical and statistical calculations. *Required*.

Must be willing to work toward perfection in all activities. *Required*.

Requires good interpersonal skill and ability to work effectively with a wide variety of people and personality types.

Bachelor's degree in engineering or quality assurance is *preferred*.

Work Environment

Office is located inside the manufacturing plant. Environment is often noisy and includes the normal side-effects of product production. Must be able to respond to problems during a 24-hour operating schedule on an on-call basis. Requires the ability to meet commitments and deadlines.

Physical Requirements

Must be physically able to operate a computer keyboard, telephone and variety of office equipment, including fax and copy machines. Must be able to hear, see and speak English with clarity. Lifting is less than 20 pounds and is infrequent.

Personal Qualities

Must enjoy a fast pace. Must be challenged by quality and productivity demands without becoming overly stressed.

Must be able to create and administer a complete program without close supervision. Must be able to concentrate on data, identify and isolate problems outside the human element as well as considering the human element. Must be able to provide error-free work without undue frustration or impatience.

Must be able to work effective as a member of a team. Must be able to "champion" programs and processes during periods of uncertainty and change.

Must enjoy providing exceptional customer service to both internal and external customers.

Must be flexible and willing to respond to emergency situations at all hours when required. A sense of humor is highly desirable.

Approval Signatures and dates.

Technical Patterned Interview

Introduction

Say, "Hello, (name), thanks for coming in. I appreciate your interest in our company. If you don't mind, I have a lot of questions for you, and I need you to answer them in a lot of detail. I'll be taking some notes, so don't worry about that. We may take about 30 minutes or so for my part. When I get finished, I'll give you a chance to ask me any questions you have, and we'll take whatever time we need to make sure everything is answered to your satisfaction. How does that sound? Okay, let's get started."

Qualifications

Tell me about your training and work experience with the Six Sigma programs.

What is your level of certification? Can you provide documentation?

Give me some examples of the types of work you did using those processes.

Would you say that your proficiency is entry level, mid level or expert level? Why?

Tell me about your courses in math and statistical process controls.

What kind of grades did you make in English? What was the highest level class you took in English?

What kind of reports and documentation do you provide on an ongoing basis?

Describe your experience, if any, with handling several projects at the same time, when they're all due at once. How did you decide what to do? How did it work out?

Have you ever had a situation where you were trying to please several people at the same time? Tell me about that. What happened?

How do you go about negotiating conflicting needs?

Has there ever been a time when you were being held to a higher standard than you thought was possible or realistic? Tell me about that.

Is there any reason you wouldn't be able to respond to an emergency situation at any time of the day or night? Are you willing to do that when needed?

What have you discovered about your work abilities and limitations?

How do you define "stress"? What do you do to relieve stress?

Tell me about your experience in dealing directly with customers.

Education and Work Experience

Please tell me about all your formal education, beginning with high school. I need months and years, please.

What was the first time you ever got paid for doing a job?

Where were you and what were you doing 10 years ago?

When did you start? Month and year.

What was your job title? Your duties?

When did you leave? Month and year.

What was your pay when you started?

What was your pay when you left?

Did you have any performance reviews while you were there? What did they say about your job performance?

Did you ever have any disciplinary notices, reprimands or counseling statements while you were there? What happened?

Were you ever put on probation for any reason?

Who was your supervisor? What was it like working for her or him?

Why did you leave?

Did you give notice? How much? Did you work through all the notice period?

Are you eligible for rehire?

What did you do next?

Repeat this sequence of questions for each period of work, unemployment or school, accounting for high school through the last or current job, or at least ten years. Take detailed notes.

Have you had any other employment of any kind during the past ten years that we haven't talked about? (*If yes, repeat the sequence of questions.*)

Decision Point:

Is the candidate technically qualified? If so, continue with the interview. If not, terminate the interview now. Say, "I really appreciate your patience in answering all my questions today. However, based on your answers, I do not believe that you are the right match for this position. Would you like me to keep your application on file in case something else comes up in the next few weeks?"

Willingness and Fit:

How many days' work did you miss in the last two years for any reason?

Have you ever had any kind of warning or disciplinary notice because of absences or tardiness from work?

Have you ever been fired or asked to leave a job for any reason?

Have you ever had a positive result, or failed a drug test that was work related?

Have you ever been disciplined or warned in any way for violation of a drug or alcohol policy at work?

Tell me about your current or last company. What kind of place was it?

Tell me about your supervisor. What did you like or not like about him or her?

Describe for me the person you think of as your model for effective management.

If you could have the absolute perfect job for you, with no restrictions, what would that job be? Why?

Do you set goals for yourself? Tell me about some of your goals. Did you achieve them? Why or why not?

What kinds of things make you look forward to getting up in the morning?

What kinds of things frustrate or make you angry at work?

Have you ever had a situation where you were part of a group, and you got your work done but the rest of the group didn't? Were you penalized because of them? What happened?

I'm going to give you some words. Please tell me why they describe you or not, and why.

Analytical	Laid back	Considerate
Fearless	Ambitious	Amiable
Driven	Fun-loving	

What led you to quality assurance work? What is it about your personality that makes you well suited for this work?

Give me an example of something in your work that you wish you had done differently? Why?

Give me an example of a time when you compromised on something you felt strongly about.

What kinds of things do you do for fun?

One last question. What else can you tell me about yourself before I make my decision?

Answer the Applicant's Questions

Make note of the questions and responses to your answers.

Cordial Close

Explain the next steps in the process. Tell the candidate about when he or she can expect to hear from you. Ask about availability for a Manager's Interview, if appropriate.

Interview Results

Decide whether the candidate is qualified and proceed through the hiring process checklist. Be sure to document everything you do, with completion dates and initials.

Hiring Right *Pat Kelley*

Blueprint Four
A Business Blueprint™ for Hiring Sales Workers

1. Complete a Job Profile, or use the following Sales Job Profile.

Sales

Race Horse or Plow Horse?

There's certainly nothing wrong with plow horses—they do the routine, repetitive work that's required with some kinds of sales jobs. But we're not just interested in plow horse-type people.

We want the thoroughbreds!

If you have been the top sales person in your region for the last three years and have at least five years' financial services sales experience, we have a compensation plan that will make you sit up and take notice.

Position requires a bachelor's degree in business, with MBA preferred. Must be licensed to sell all financial services products. Pre-employment and drug tests required.

Apply on-line at www.mycompany.com.

Equal Opportunity Employer

---

2. If job is to be advertised, develop a newspaper ad, post the job internally and/or on the company's Web site.

3. Begin networking. Contact professional associations, business and professional associates, vendors, former employees, etc. Allow at

least two weeks for this process before contacting search agencies or placing ads.

4. Do some "shopping" in your market area. Visit other companies that offer products and services similar to yours. Shop the providers and their sales staff. When you meet someone who impresses you, give them your card and a sales pitch.

5. Conduct internal interviews with current sales staff, as appropriate.

6. Ask your customers whom they have worked with, and have been impressed with, at competing companies. Ask them to make a call or two on your behalf, with instructions to have potential candidates contact you directly.

7. Contact a professional search agency that specializes in your industry, preferably someone who works on a contingency basis. Consider giving an exclusive to your recruiter of choice. Allow six weeks to six months for this process. Be as candid as possible with your search consultant. The more information she has, the better she will be able to match candidates to your position.

8. As part of the preliminary screening process, require that applicants complete an employment application, as well as sending you their resume. Require that applicants you are considering for an interview complete a personality questionnaire.

9. If you are interviewing from referrals, conduct a credit check and background check prior to the first interview, but *after* the application has been completed and signed.

10. If you are using a search consultant, require the completed application, personality profile, credit and background checks *prior* to an on-site visit.

11. Conduct a comprehensive telephone interview, unless applicants

are within two hours' driving time. See Chapter Two, Recruiting and Screening Applicants. During the telephone interview, request that applicants have colleges and universities forward *directly to you* official transcripts verifying any and all claimed degrees.

12. Have the search consultant send all on-site interviewees a packet of information about your company. Include Chamber of Commerce information about the local community, including schools, cultural and recreational opportunities. Include the latest Sunday Real Estate section of the most recent newspaper.

13. Have search consultants complete a preliminary reference check verifying dates of employment, job titles, pay, reasons for leaving and rehire eligibility for all positions listed on the employment application or resume. In addition, personally speak to at least two professional references yourself, preferably former supervisors.

14. Schedule on-site interviews. See the following Patterned Interview and On-site Candidate Interview Schedule and Report forms.

15. Complete a comprehensive reference check on potential final candidates. (See Chapter 4.) ***Do not skip this critical step.***

16. Evaluate all final candidates for the best match. Invite the first choice back for a second visit, this time with his or her spouse. See the Second Visit Schedule for an example. Be prepared to discuss preliminary financial goals during this visit. If you are using a search consultant, ask for a reaction to a preliminary offer before it is discussed with the candidate.

17. Host the first choice candidate and his/her spouse for the second visit.

18. Evaluate the results of the second visit. Decide whether or not to make a formal job offer. If no, inform the candidate either personally or through the search consultant that an offer will not be made. No reason needs to be given—at this level it's simply a matter of "fit" or "not a fit."

19. If you will be making a formal job offer, draft a written offer letter. Review it with executives for approval, if needed. Fax a draft to the search consultant, if appropriate, for feedback. Make changes needed if you agree.

20. Telephone the candidate. Using the written offer letter as a guide, make a conditional job offer, contingent upon final completion of all pre-employment requirements, including receipt of transcripts, final references and drug test. Ask for a commitment within no more than a few days —"Would July 12 be a good start date?" *(Be careful to avoid making any promises, especially if you are an at-will employer.)* Tell the candidate you will be mailing the offer letter and he or she should be prepared to give notice to his/her employer immediately after receiving the formal offer letter. Ask the candidate to let you know when he/she has given notice, and to confirm the start date.

21. Upon acceptance of the formal offer, schedule the candidate for a drug test. Complete final references. Review drug test results.

22. Call the applicant to confirm the offer, schedule a house hunting visit with his/her spouse, and begin making relocation arrangements. Schedule a start date.

23. Notify unsuccessful applicants that the job has been filled. Send thank-you notes to everyone who sent you a referral and to all the candidates who interviewed on-site. Be sure the search consultant sends a thank you to all their referrals.

24. Meet with internal staff to announce the planned start date and to discuss any changes they should expect.

Note: If the final candidates are local, some of the schedule can be modified. For example, a drug test can be scheduled as soon as the second visit is confirmed, and no house-hunting trip will be necessary.

Forms Needed

- Completed Job Profile
- Patterned Interview
- Telephone Reference Check
- Written Reference Check
- On-Site Candidate interview Schedule and Report
- Second Interview Schedule
- Other new hire form as needed

Sales Job Profile

Primary Duties:

Sells a wide range of investment products to company clients.

Develops leads, referrals and prospects through business and professional relationships and indirect contacts.

Qualifies prospects and sells the appropriate products.

Follows up with referrals from branch staff throughout the company. Qualifies the prospects, diagnoses their needs and sells the appropriate products.

Represents the company in a variety of business and non-profit organizations to build business.

Mentors branch staff to help them increase qualified referrals and possibly grow into a sales position.

Recommends new products and services that will add to available products and maintain competitive position as the market leader.

Produces a variety of monthly sales reports that track progress toward goals, budget, increases and decreases, etc.

Secondary Duties:

Other duties as assigned.

Performance Standards:

Achieves or exceeds all sales goals.

60% of sales are from personal sources. All sales are to financially qualified clients.

40% of sales are from branch referrals. All sales are to financially qualified clients.

Holds officer or Board level positions in two major company approved service or professional organizations.

10% growth in qualified referrals per branch per year. Two new staff promotions to sales each year.

Increases market dominance by 5% per year with products that meet company profit guidelines.

Must be able to speak, read and write English with clarity and perform math with the proficiency required by the position.

Knowledge, Skills and Aptitudes

Minimum five years sales experience in a financial services environment is required. Bachelor's degree in business administration is required or much be completed within two years of acceptance of position. MBA preferred. Proficiency in Microsoft Excel and Access, and related operating systems, is required.

All required financial services sales licenses must be current and must be maintained current with no expiration. Requires effective interpersonal skills and ability to work effectively with a variety of people and personality styles.

Work Environment

Requires up to 75% of time outside the office meeting with clients and participating in business-building association activities. Some meetings will be in the evenings and on weekends. Requires regular contact and follow-up with all branches, sometimes requiring overnight travel.

Physical Requirements

Must be able physically to operate a computer keyboard, telephone and variety of office equipment, including fax and copy machines. Must be able to hear, see, and speak English with clarity. Must be able to travel to and from business locations and stay overnight when required. Normal lifting is less than five pounds and infrequent. Setting up for presentations sometimes requires handling computer and peripheral equipment, bending, stooping, reaching, hauling and lifting up to 30 pounds occasionally.

Personal Qualities

Must enjoy a fast pace. Must be challenged by challenged by meeting goals and by quality and productivity demands without becoming overly stressed.

Must be able to work without close supervision. Must be able to focus on data, identify and isolate customer needs and offer appropriate product or service. Must be able to provide error-free work without undue frustration or impatience.

Must be able to work effectively with a wide range of people and personality types, building effective relationships and referrals. Must genuinely enjoy helping other people meet their financial goals.

Must enjoy providing exceptional service to facilitate repeat business and referrals.

Sales Patterned Interview

"Hello, (name), thanks for coming in. I appreciate your interest in (company name.) If you don't mind, I have a lot of questions for you, and I need you to answer them in a lot of detail. I'll be taking a lot of notes, so don't let that distract you. We may take about 30 minutes or so for my part. When I get finished, I'll give you a chance to ask me any questions you have, and we'll take whatever time we need to make sure everything is answered to your satisfaction. If that's all okay, let's get started."

Qualifications:

Have you had five years of sales experience in financial services?

Do you have a Bachelor's degree in business? What was your GPA? Will you have your schools send me certified copies of your transcripts, please?

Have you completed your MBA? When and where?

Tell me about your professional licenses. Are you current with all your continuing education?

Give me a list of all the products and services you're qualified to sell.

Have you met your sales goals in each of the last three years? Tell me about those goals, please.

What kinds of operating system have you used?

What kind of time management system do you use?

How do you go about scheduling your work so that you're able to meet all your client needs?

Do you have any preferences about the kind of people you work with?

Briefly tell me about your financial services experience in areas other than sales.

Briefly tell me about your sales experience in areas other than financial services.

Education and Work Experience:

What was your first job after you graduated from college? (Alternative question: Where were you and what were you doing ten years ago?)

When did you start? Month and year.

When did you leave? Month and year.

What was your job title? Your duties?

What was your pay when you started?

What was your pay when you left?

Did you have any performance reviews while you were there?

What did they say about your job performance?

Did you ever have any disciplinary notices, reprimands or counseling for any reason while you were there? What happened?

Were you ever put on probation for any reason?

Who was your supervisor? What was it like working for her?

Why did you leave? Did you give notice? Did you work through the notice?

Are you eligible for rehire?

What did you do next?

Repeat this sequence of questions for each period of work, unemployment or school, accounting for high school or college through the last or current job, or at least ten years.

Decision Point:

Is the candidate technically qualified? If so, continue with the interview. If not, terminate the interview now. Say, (applicant's name), "I really appreciate your coming in today, but based on your answers it is my judgment that you're not a good match for this position. I enjoyed meeting you, and hope you'll periodically update your file so that we can consider you for future positions."

Willingness and Fit:

What led you to choose sales for a career? Has it been what you expected? Any surprises?

What were your gross earnings in each of the last three years?

Describe your compensation program for me.

What have you learned about yourself from having been sales? Have there been any surprises?

Tell me about (current or last company name). What kind of place was it.

Describe the culture for me.

What did you accomplish there?

What would you change about your experience at that company? Why?

What would you change about your experience at (another company)?

Since so much of your work depends on referrals from people who do not work directly for you, how do you get them to give you the referrals you need?

Have you ever had any conflicts of any kind with the people at work? Tell me about that.

Give me some words that describe your personality, and give me some examples that illustrate that.

How did your last two managers describe you?

Your co-workers? How do they describe you?

Are you about where you thought you would be at this point in your career? Why or why not?

How do you prefer to be managed? Any "pet peeves"?

What kinds of things frustrate you make you angry at work?

As you look at your work experience so far, is there anything you'd like to do over? Why?

Tell me about the worst mistake you've made during your career so far. What did you learn about yourself?

What kinds of things do you do for fun? How do you spend your spare time?

What kinds of things are you doing in the community? In a professional association?

Have you ever been fired or asked to leave a job for any reason? Have you ever had a positive result, or failed a drug test that was work related?

Have you ever been disciplined or warned in any way for violation of a drug or alcohol policy at work?

Have you ever been disciplined or warned in any way for having a weapon at work, or for fighting or violence of any kind at work?

Have you ever filed for bankruptcy, or had a foreclosure or lien of any kind filed against you? Tell me about that.

How is your credit today? How do you know?

Final question: What else can you tell me about yourself before I make my decision?

Answer the Applicant's Questions

Note the questions for the file.

Cordial Close

Explain the next steps in the process.

Interview Results

Decide whether the candidate is qualified and proceed through the hiring process checklist. Be sure to document everything you do, with completion dates and initials.

Sales Candidate Interview Schedule and Review

To: Distribution

From: Director of Human Resources

Subject: Sales Candidate Visit

Janice Jones has been scheduled for an on-site interview on Tuesday, June 19, 2014. Her schedule is listed below. Please let me know immediately if you have a schedule conflict.

When your interview is completed, please escort the candidate to her next appointment. Please be on time! Complete the attached evaluation and return it to me by the end of the day.

Thanks very much for your help. Let me know if you have any questions.

Janice Jones Interview Schedule

Tuesday, June 19

8:30 a.m. HR Director Introduction

9:00 a.m. President, Financial Services, Interview

10:30 a.m.   Branch Manager interview

11:00 a.m.   Branch Manager interview

12 Noon   Group lunch, location, list of branch staff participants

2:00 p.m. Facility tour, meet other company staff, including President, if possible.

3:00 p.m. HR Director wrap-up

Interview Results:

Candidate appears to be qualified for the position (refer to Job Profile)   Yes   No   Explain: _____

_____

Candidate appears to be a "fit" for our culture and work environment.
           Yes   No   Explain: _____

_____

Candidate's strengths: _____

_____

Areas for concern: _____

_____

Recommend hire: Yes   No   Explain: _____

_____

Interview conducted by: (name and job title) _____   Date _____

Return this evaluation form to the Director of HR by the end of business today. Thanks very much for your help!

Sales Candidate Offer Letter

Date

Name and Address

Dear first name,

I am delighted to confirm in writing the offer of employment we discussed today by telephone. Here are the details:

Your job title will be Financial Sales Specialist, reporting to the President, Financial Services. You have agreed that your tentative start date will be July 17, 2014. Your pay will be based on 100% commissions, in accordance with the attached Compensation Agreement. As we discussed, for benefits and pay stability purposes, your draw against commission will be $2,000 bi-weekly

This offer of employment is contingent upon satisfactory completion of pre-hire drug, background and credit checks, as well as employment references and receipt of your certified college transcripts and certificates of completion.

You will be eligible to enroll in Company medical, life and dental insurance upon completion of your eligibility period, normally 90 days after employment. You will receive an enrollment packet and instructions prior to your eligibility date. Your 401(k) eligibility requires six full months of employment, and FMLA eligibility requires one full year of employment. Please refer to the official program documents for full details.

In addition, the Company will support your continuing professional education by reimbursing you for all completed and qualified CPE programs.

On your first day of employment, please report to the Human Resources Department, located at (insert location) at 8:00 a.m. You will participate in a mandatory New Employee Orientation at that time. During the orientation, you will complete your new-hire paperwork. You must bring your approved identification documents with you. A list is enclosed. For the orientation, you may park in visitor parking, located near the front entrance of the building. Future parking will be assigned by your supervisor.

We are fully convinced that you are the right person for this job, (insert first name). This offer, however, does not provide a guarantee of future employment. This company is and will continue to be an at-will employer.

Please confirm your acceptance of this offer by calling me at (phone number) no later than (two days after expected receipt of the letter.) If you do not respond by that date, the offer will be withdrawn.

Let me know if you have any questions. We believe (company name) is a great place to work, and that you will be a terrific addition to the team. We look forward to seeing you on July 17!

Yours truly,

Encl: I-9 Documents List

    Facilities Map

    Compensation Program for Sales Associates

    Employee Handbook

Sales New Employee Orientation Schedule

Week One:

Complete new hire paperwork including Employee Handbook and Code of Conduct. Initial and date when complete.

Receive Benefits materials and review benefits. Initial and date when complete.

Complete New Employee Orientation Program. Include Certificate of Completion for the personnel file.

Receive tour of facility, meet co-workers, receive keys, learn timekeeping system. Initial and date when complete.

Review Orientation Checklist, understand responsibility for properly completing Checklist. Review job description and performance standards. Initial and date when complete.

Receive operating system authorization. Set up in the system, enter secure password. Initial and date when complete.

Learn where procedures manuals and forms are kept. Study department and Company policies and procedures. Correctly answer random questions about policies and procedures. Initial and date when complete.

Begin becoming familiar with sales forms and procedures. Receive list of current clients and begin making telephone introductions.

Week Two:

Review first week with supervisor. Ask questions as needed. Initial and date when complete.

Continue building familiarity and proficiency with policies and procedures, and sales forms and procedures.

Continue telephone introductions to key clients.

Schedule and participate in meetings with key interface staff in other departments to discuss their goals and needs. Initial and date when complete.

Begin routine job responsibilities.

Review second week with supervisor, ask questions. Initial and date when complete.

Week Three:

Review second week with supervisor, ask questions. Initial and date when complete.

If necessary, complete meetings with key interface staff in other departments. Initial and date when complete.

Continue normal job duties.

Complete telephone introductions with key clients. Initial and date when complete.

Begin meeting new clients, including referrals from Branch offices.

File completed form in the employee's personnel file.

Blueprint Five
A Business Blueprint™ for Hiring Management Staff

1. Complete a Job Profile, or use the following Management Job Profile.

2. Begin networking. Contact professional associations, business and professional associates, vendors, former employees, etc. Allow at least two weeks for this process before contacting search agencies or placing ads.

3. Ask your customers whom they have worked with, and have been impressed with, at competing companies. Ask them to make a call or two on your behalf, with instructions to have potential candidates contact you directly.

4. Contact a professional search agency that specializes in your industry, preferably someone who works on a commission system. If this is a senior executive position, consider hiring an executive search firm or giving an exclusive to your recruiter of choice. Allow six weeks to six months for this process. Be as candid as possible with your search consultant. The more information she has, the better she will be able to match candidates to your position.

5. As part of the preliminary screening process, require that applicants complete an employment application, as well as sending you their resume. Require that applicants you are considering for an interview complete a validated Personality

Questionnaire (See Resources.) Most profiles are now available on-line at very reasonable costs.

6. If you are interviewing from referrals, conduct a credit check and background check prior to the first interview, after the application has been completed and signed.

7. If you are using a search consultant, require the completed application, personality profile, credit and background checks prior to an on-site visit.

8. Conduct a comprehensive telephone interview, unless applicants are within two hours' driving time. See Chapter Two, Recruiting and Screening Applicants.) During the telephone interview, request that applicants have colleges and universities forward official transcripts directly to you, to verify any claimed degrees.

9. Send applicants you have telephone interviewed (or have search consultant send) a packet of information about your company. If the applicant is out of town, include Chamber of Commerce information about the local community, including schools, cultural and recreational opportunities. Include the Sunday Real Estate section of the most recent newspaper.

10. On potential final candidates, complete a preliminary reference check (or have the search consultant do so) verifying the dates of employment, job titles, pay, reasons for leaving and rehire eligibility for all positions listed on the employment application or resume. In addition, speak to at least two professional references, preferably former supervisors.

11. Schedule on-site interviews. See the following Patterned Interview and On-Site Candidate Interview Schedule and Report.)

12. Conduct on-site interviews.

13. Complete a comprehensive reference check on final candidates. See Chapter Four. ***Do not skip this critical step!***

14. Evaluate all final candidates for the best match. Invite the first choice back for a second visit, this time with his/her spouse. See the attached Second Visit Schedule. Be prepared to discuss preliminary financial goals during this visit. If you are using a search consultant, ask for a reaction to a preliminary offer before it is discussed with the candidate.

15. Host the first choice candidate and his/her spouse for the second visit.

16. Evaluate the results of the second visit. Decide whether or not to make a formal job offer. If no, inform the candidate either personally or through the search consultant that an offer will not be made. No reason needs to be given—at this level it's simply a matter of "fit" or "not a fit."

17. If you will be making a formal job offer, draft a written offer letter. Review it with executives for approval if needed, and fax a draft to the search consultant, if appropriate.

18. Telephone the candidate. Using the written offer letter as a guide, make a conditional job offer, contingent upon final completion of all pre-employment requirements, including receipt of transcripts, final references and drug test. Ask for a commitment—"Would July 12 be a good start date?"—within no more than a few days. Tell the candidate you will be mailing the offer letter and he/she should be prepared to give notice to his/her employer immediately after receiving the formal offer letter.

19. Upon acceptance of the formal offer, schedule the candidate for a drug test. Complete final references. Review drug test results.

20. Call applicant with confirmed offer, discuss relocation details, begin making relocation arrangements. Schedule confirmed start date.

21. Notify unsuccessful applicants that the job has been filled. Send thank-you notes to everyone who sent you a referral.

22. Meet with internal staff to announce a planned start date.

Note: If the final candidates are local, some of this schedule can be modified. For example, a drug test can be schedule as soon as the second visit is confirmed.

Forms Needed

- Completed Job Profile
- Patterned Interview form for Management Candidate
- Telephone Reference Check
- Written Reference Check
- On-site Candidate Interview Schedule and Report
- Second Interview Schedule
- Other new hire forms as needed

Management Job Profile

Primary Duties

Manages a department of 12 employees responsible for providing sales, services and support to field customers. 40%

Hires, trains and evaluates employees. Schedules time off, weekly work rotations, work positions, training time. Coaches and counsels employees to meet job standards. 20%

Prepares weekly and monthly reports to supervisor, detailing department results. Submits monthly budget variance report. Prepares and submits annual operating budget for approval; manages within budget during the year. 15%
Personally meets with key customers to facilitate large sales and/or long-term relationships. Participates in negotiations as required to close sales. 15%

Serves on one or more company-wide task groups for product development, technology or process improvement. 10%

Secondary Duties
Other duties as assigned or required.

Performance Standards

Department meets established standards for call waiting time, accurate handling of issues and requests, problem resolution, lost calls, etc.

100% coverage at all times. Turnover less than 5% per year. Performance reviews and pay actions are on time. All department performance standards are met.

All reports and submissions are accurate and on time. Data is useful and valid for strategic planning purposes. Manages within department budget.

Relationships with other department managers are good, with no problems noted. Meets commitments for project work. Quality of work is professional and reflects forward thinking and state-of-the-art processes.

All users evaluate support as "meets requirements" or better. No complaints received.

Must be able to speak, read and write English with clarity, and perform math at the high school graduate level. Proficiency in Spanish is also preferred.

Knowledge, Skills and Attitudes

Minimum five years' supervisory experience in a customer service center environment is required. Bachelor's degree in business administration, accounting or finance is required. Proficiency in Microsoft Office products and related operating systems is required. Proficiency with Centrex C/S systems is required. Must be able to deal effectively with competing priorities, properly handle customer and employee situations, develop and implement effective project plans. Must be patient, customer and employee oriented, able to function effectively in crisis situations. Must be a good leader, as well as a good manager. Must exhibit and model the good sales and customer service behaviors required of CS associates.

Work Environment

Position is situated in a busy office where a variety of work is done. Teamwork is required to accomplish tasks on a timely basis. Work area is open and noisy with a variety of conversations and operating equipment working at all times. Priorities can change quickly, with very little notice. High levels of quality and productivity are required. Attire is business casual.

Physical Requirements

Must be physically able to operate a computer keyboard, telephone and variety of office equipment, including fax and copy machines. Must be able to hear, see, and speak English with clarity. Lifting is less than five pounds and infrequent.

Personal Qualities

Must enjoy a fast pace. Must be challenged by quality and productivity demands without becoming overly stressed.

Must be able to work alone for brief periods without close supervision. Must be able to concentrate on data; identify and isolate problems. Must be able to provide error-free work without undue frustration or impatience.

Must be able to work effectively in a team environment, where employees, peers and customers are involved in problem-solving. Must be able to lead without taking control, to bring out the best in the group, and to resolve interpersonal problems and issues without loss of productivity.

Must enjoy providing exceptional customer service, both to internal and external customers.

Must be flexible. A sense of humor is highly desirable.

Signature approvals

Management Patterned Interview

"Hello (name), thanks for coming in. I appreciate your interest in (Company name). If you don't mind, I have a lot of questions for you, and I need you to answer them in a lot of detail. I'll be taking some notes, so don't let that bother you. We may take about an hour or so for my part. When I get finished, I'll give you a chance to ask me any questions you have, and we'll take whatever time we need to make sure everything is answered to your satisfaction. Shall we get started?"

Qualifications Questions

Have you had five years of supervisory experience in a customer service center environment?

Tell me about your training and experience with Centrex Customer Service operating systems.

Tell me about your training and work experience with the Microsoft Office suite of products. Which version do you use?

Give me some examples of the types of work you did/do using those products.

How many people have you supervised at one time? For how long have you been a supervisor?

Describe your experience with handling several projects at the same time, when they're all due at once. How did you decide what to do? How did it work out?

Tell me about an experience where you were in charge of a project from conception to implementation. How did you manage that? What were the problems? The results?

What kind of time management system do you use?

Have you ever had a situation where you were trying to please several people at the same time? Tell me about that. What happened?

Tell me about the kinds of management reporting you have done. How often? What were the reports used for?

How do you handle performance management issues with employees? Give me an example, please.

Tell me how you go about the process of hiring a new employees.

Have you ever had to terminate an employee? What happened?

Has an employee ever filed a complaint against you? Tell me about that.

Do you have any preferences about the kind of people you work with?

Education and Work Experience

Please tell me about all your formal education, beginning with high school. Did you graduate? Will you have your college send me a certified copy of your transcript?

Alternate Question: Where were you and what were you doing ten years ago?

What was your first job after you graduated from College? When did you start? (Month and Year)

When did you leave there? Last day worked? (Month/Year)

What was your job title? Your duties?

What was your pay when you started? What was your pay when you left?

Did you have any performance reviews while you were there? What did they say about your job performance?

Did you ever have any disciplinary notices, reprimands or counseling statements while you were there? What happened?

Were you ever put on probation for any reason?

Who was your supervisor? What was it like working for him/her?

Why did you leave? Did you give notice?

Are you eligible for rehire?

What did you do next?
(Repeat this sequence of questions for each period of work, unemployment or school, accounting for high school or last time school was attended, through the last job. Take notes on a separate page.)

Have you had any other employment of any kind that we haven't talked about? (If yes, repeat the sequence of questions.)

Tell me about the job-related training you've had in the past ten years or so.

Decision Point:

Is the candidate technically qualified? If yes, continue with the interview. If not, terminate the interview now. Say, "Applicant's name), I really appreciate your coming in today but, based on your answers, I do not believe you are a good match for this position.

Would you like me to keep your application on file in case something else comes up in the next few weeks?"

Notes:

Willingness and Fit
Tell me about (Company name). What kind of place was it?

Describe the culture for me.

What would you change about your experience at (that

Company?) Why?

How about at (another Company)?

Give me some words that describe your personality.

What do (did) your direct reports have to say about you?

How about your last two managers? How did they describe you?

Are you about where you thought you would be at this point in

your career? Why or why not?

Do you set goals for yourself? Tell me about some of your goals.

Did you achieve them? Why or why not?

What kinds of things make you look forward to getting up in the mornings?

What have you learned about yourself from having been a supervisor?

Were there any surprises?

How do you describe your management style?

How do you prefer to be managed? Any "pet peeves"?

What kinds of things frustrate or make you angry at work?

As you look at your work experience so far, is there anything you'd like to do over? Why?

Tell me about the worst mistake you've made during your career. What did you learn about yourself?

Tell me about your best accomplishments. Go ahead, brag.

What kinds of things do you do for fun? How do you spend your spare time?

What kinds of things are you doing in the community?

In a professional association?

What are the last two books you read? What did you learn from them?

What newspapers and magazines do you read regularly?

Have you ever been fired or asked to leave a job for any reason?

Have you ever had a positive result, or failed a drug test that was work related?

Have you ever been disciplined or warned in any way for violation of a drug or alcohol policy at work?

Have you ever been disciplined or warned in any way for having a weapon at work, or for fighting or violence of any kind at work?

Have you ever filed for bankruptcy, or had a foreclosure of lien of any kind filed against you? Tell me about that, please.

How is your credit today? How do you know?

Final question: What else can you tell me about yourself before I make my decision?

Hiring Right   Pat Kelley

Answer the Applicant's Questions

Cordial Close

Explain the next steps in the process.

Interview Results

Is the candidate qualified?   Yes No   If no, why not?

Referred to Hiring Manager for interview? Yes No   Date Referred?

References Completed Date   Acceptable?   Yes No
    (Attach form)

Transcripts Received Date   Acceptable?   Yes No

Credit Check Completed Date   Acceptable?   Yes No

Background Check Completed Date   Acceptable?   Yes No

Drug Test Results   Acceptable?   Yes No

Personality Profile Complete Date   Acceptable?   Yes No

Conditional Offer of Employment Made Date   Details

    Telephone

    Mail

    Job Title

    Reports To

    Starting Pay

Pat Kelley *Hiring Right*

Location

Offer Accepted Date   Start Date

Management Candidate Interview Schedule and Review

The first part of this Schedule is the same as the Sales candidate schedule, with minor modifications as needed.

Interview Schedule:

Arrives our city: Date, time, airline and flight number, met by (name) or (rental car)

Hotel: Name, location, confirmed reservation number

Tuesday, June 19

8:30 a.m. HR Director will pick up at hotel and bring to office.

9:00 a.m. President or Chief Operating Officer interview

10:00 a.m.   Compliance Manager interview

11:00 a.m.   Director of Sales interview

12 Noon   Group lunch, location, list of participants

2:00 p.m. Team meeting with Customer Service Staff

3:00 p.m. HR Director wrap-up and drive to airport for return trip, airline and flight number

Interview Results:

Same as Sales

Management Candidate Second Interview and Spouse Visit Schedule

Thomas Thompson has been scheduled for a second interview and spouse (name) visit on Thursday, Friday and Saturday, June 27-19. His schedule is shown below. Please let me know immediately if you have a schedule conflict.

Please be on time for your meetings, and remember to escort the candidate to his next appointment. Thanks very much for your help. Please let me know if you have any questions.

Interview Schedule:

Arrives our city: Date, time, airline and flight number, rental car details

Hotel: Name, location, confirmed reservation number

Thursday, June 27

4:30 p.m.   Arrive at hotel and check in.

5:30 p.m. Realtor (name, contact information) to meet the Thompsons at the hotel and take them to dinner. Discuss real estate preferences.

Friday, June 28

8:00 a.m. Breakfast at the hotel, the Thompsons and Director of Sales

9:00 a.m. Realtor picks up Mrs. Thompson at the hotel. Candidate returns to the office with the Director of Sales.

10:00 a.m.   Director of Sales informal tour of facilities, say hello to CS Manager peers, team members.

12 Noon   Lunch with candidate, list of participants. Restaurant details, location.

2:00 p.m. Director of Sales returns candidate to hotel or another location to meet spouse and realtor. Remainder of day is open for community tours and/or real estate visits.

Saturday, June 29

AM-PM   Candidate and spouse continue real estate search with realtor, or free time.

6:00 p.m. Director of Sales and President, with their spouses, take Candidate and spouse to dinner. Conditional offer may be made here, verbal only.

Sunday, June 30

9:30 a.m. Candidate and spouse return to airport for 11:00 a.m. flight, airline, flight number.

Contact Numbers;

Director of Sales, Human Resources Director, Realtor, Hotel, Airline, Candidate, Candidate Spouse

Management Candidate Offer Letter

Dear (Name

I am delighted to confirm in writing the offer of employment we discussed today by telephone. Here are the details:

Your job title will be Customer Service Manager, reporting to (insert name and title). You have agreed that your tentative start date will be August 1. Your starting pay will be $2,333.33 per pay period (bi-weekly). For your convenience, that computes to $56,000 on an annual basis. You will be immediately eligible to participate in the Management Incentive Plan, with your first year participation pro-rated for the period actually worked. Future pay increases and bonus eligibility will be based on your job performance and Company policy.

In addition, the Company will support your relocation to the (city) area as follows:

- We will pay the full cost of moving your household goods in accordance with Company policy.
- We will pay your temporary living expenses for up to 45 days, while your family relocates.
- If necessary, we will pay for the actual costs of a house-hunting trip for you and your family, for up to five days.
- We will pay you a $5,000 relocation bonus, due on your first day of employment, or the closing of your Tulsa home, whichever is first.

Hiring Right   *Pat Kelley*

You will be eligible to enroll in the company medical, life and dental insurance, upon completion of your eligibility period. In your case, that will be November 1. You will receive an enrollment packet and instructions prior to your eligibility date. Your paid-time-off benefits will also begin accruing on the first day of your employment. Both 401(k) and FMLA eligibility require one full year of employment.

Continue the offer letter as in the Sales Candidate Offer Letter.

Yours truly,

Management Orientation Checklist

Modify and use the Technical or Sales New Employee Checklist

Resources for Additional Information about Hiring

The very best source of information about hiring, or about any aspect of Human Resources Management, is the ***Society for Human Resources Management***, or ***SHRM***. On the Internet, go to SHRM.org. By mail: 1800 Duke Street, Alexandria, Virginia 22314. By telephone: 800-283-7475.

This is where you will find professional staff who support the 300,000 professionals working in HR management in every conceivable industry throughout the world. They sponsor dozens of conferences, workshops, programs and presentations every year. They publish magazines, newsletters, white papers and books. They lobby Congress for laws that support the best interest of employers and employees alike. For their members, they will do research and answer specific questions. They have an on-line bookstore featuring hundreds, if not thousands, of resources in the field of Human Resources Management.

One of the most important things SHRM does is sponsor the Human Resources Certification Institute, HRCI, which provides resources for the in-depth study of HR. Their Certifications, Professional in Human Resources (PHR) and Senior Professional in Human Resources (SPHR) have boosted the professionalism (and the earnings) of millions of HR staffers throughout the world.

In addition, once you become a SHRM member, you will be automatically added to the mailing lists of dozens of vendors for every conceivable HR service or supply.

Remember to check out your local chapter of SHRM to meet other area HR professionals in a variety of industries, including the staffing and placement professionals. Become a volunteer for this group and enjoy the benefits of meeting and networking with area HR professionals. Both the state and local chapters have outstanding monthly meetings and programs, and most also have valuable conferences and other learning experiences.

For *personality testing resources*, including legal guidelines, go to the *American Psychological Association, or APA*. On the Web, find them at APA.org. By mail: 750 First Street NE, Washington, DC 20002. By telephone: 800-374-2721.

This is where you'll find thousands of resources dealing with legal issues, using tests in the hiring process, and so on. If you are considering using personality testing in your hiring process, I strongly recommend you spend time browsing through this site and perhaps even ordering some of the available materials.

If you have read this book, you know that I encourage the use of personality testing in the hiring process. However, you cannot simply go to an office supply center and purchase test kits off the shelf. To be legal, your tests must be *valid* and *predictive for your specific jobs*. Using tests that have not been validated would be a disservice both to your company and to the applicants.

The APA has dozens of resources that will help you with this process.

You can also directly contact *the Equal Employment Opportunity Commission, EEOC,* at www.EEOC.gov.

Contacting the EEOC directly can be somewhat intimidating if you are concerned about a possible compliance audit. However, in the author's personal experience, the EEOC staff are very professional and extremely helpful in every aspect of compliance. They will help with the educational and research tools you need, and will coach you in every step of the compliance process.

In addition, if your company is found to be in non-compliance, most EEOC staff are willing to work with you to become compliant as quickly and painlessly as possible.

Remember to check the U.S. Department of Labor for the latest DOL rules, law updates, and free resources. Your state also has a State Department of Labor with the same information. The easiest way to access all this free information is to use the Internet. Check out www.USDOL.gov or a similar site. For State DOL resources, try www.ARDOL.gov and substitute your state's abbreviation.

Finally, the author of this book is happy to answer any questions you have about the hiring process and other HR issues. Contact her at www.patkelleyauthor.net.

Good luck with your hiring!

About the author

Pat Kelley worked more than 43 years in the career field of Human Resources Management before retiring to write full time.

She worked in banking, communications, manufacturing and food processing. Her first job was secretary to the Assistant Vice President of Employee Relations, but she quickly began moving up and in fewer than ten years was Director of Human Resources for the state's largest bank.

During her distinguished career, Ms. Kelley earned her Master's degree in adult education and taught management and human resources classes for Webster University's Fort Smith, Arkansas campus for more than fifteen years. She earned certification as a Senior Professional in Human Resources, and in 2008 was named recipient of the Lifetime Achievement Award from the Arkansas Society of Human Resource Management.

In addition to the non-fiction books **Hiring Right: A Business Blueprint for Lower Turnover and Higher Profits** and **Lessons Learned: Cases from 43 Years in Human Resources**, Ms. Kelley is also the author of three fiction books.

She lives in eastern Oklahoma and makes frequent appearances at book clubs, writers conferences and management seminars. Her Web site is at www.patkelleyauthor.net.

www.ingramcontent.com/pod-product-compliance
Lightning Source LLC
Chambersburg PA
CBHW051644170526
45167CB00001B/326